THE
MIST
OF
MERCY

Spiritual Warfare and Purgatory

By Anne, a lay apostle

THE
MIST
OF
MERCY

By Anne, a lay apostle

ISBN: 978-1-933684-24-6

Library of Congress Number: applied for

Publisher: Direction for Our Times
                  9000 West 81st Street
                  Justice, Illinois 60458

                  708-496-9300
                  www.directionforourtimes.org

Direction for Our Times is a 501(c)(3) tax-exempt organization.

Manufactured in the United States of America.

Graphic design and stained glass art by:
          Chris Deschaine
          www.braintrustdesign.com

How to Pray the Rosary information, the image of St. Michael and the image of Our Lady Immaculate are used with permission. Copyright © Congregation of Marians of the Immaculate Conception, Stockbridge, MA 01263. www.marian.org.

Painting of *Jesus Christ the Returning King* by Janusz Antosz

Direction for Our Times wishes to manifest its complete obedience and submission of mind and heart to the final and definitive judgment of the Magisterium of the Catholic Church and the local Ordinary regarding the supernatural character of the messages received by Anne, a lay apostle.

In this spirit, the messages of Anne, a lay apostle, have been submitted to her bishop, Most Reverend Leo O'Reilly, Bishop of Kilmore, Ireland, and to the Vatican Congregation for the Doctrine of the Faith for formal examination. In the meantime Bishop O'Reilly has given permission for their publication.

Table of Contents

Introduction

Dear Reader,

I am a wife, mother of six, and a Secular Franciscan.

At the age of twenty, I was divorced for serious reasons and with pastoral support in this decision. In my mid-twenties I was a single parent, working and bringing up a daughter. As a daily Mass communicant, I saw my faith as sustaining and had begun a journey toward unity with Jesus, through the Secular Franciscan Order or Third Order.

My sister travelled to Medjugorje and came home on fire with the Holy Spirit. After hearing of her beautiful pilgrimage, I experienced an even more profound conversion. During the following year I experienced various levels of deepened prayer, including a dream of the Blessed Mother, where she asked me if I would work for Christ. During the dream she showed me that this special spiritual work would mean I would be separated from others in the world. She actually showed me my extended family and how I would be separated from them. I told her that I did not care. I would do anything asked of me.

Shortly after, I became sick with endometriosis. I have been sick ever since, with one thing or another. My sicknesses are always the types that mystify doctors in the beginning. This is part of the cross and I mention it because so many suffer in this way. I was told by my doctor that I would never conceive children. As a single parent, this did not concern me as I assumed it was God's will. Soon after, I met a wonderful man. My first marriage had been annulled and we married and conceived five children.

Spiritually speaking, I had many experiences that included what I now know to be interior locutions. These moments were beautiful and the words still stand out firmly in my heart, but I did not get excited because I was busy offering up illnesses and exhaustion. I took it as a matter of course that Jesus had to work hard to sustain me as He had given me a lot to handle. In looking back, I see that He was preparing me to do His work. My preparation period was long, difficult and not very exciting. From the outside, I think people thought, man, that woman has bad luck. From the inside, I saw that while my sufferings were painful and long lasting, my little family was growing in love, in size and in wisdom, in the sense that my husband and I certainly understood what was important and what was not important. Our continued crosses did that for us.

Various circumstances compelled my husband and me to move with our children far from my loved ones. I offered this up and must say it is the most difficult thing I have had to contend with. Living in exile brings many beautiful opportunities to align with Christ's will; however, you have to continually remind yourself that you are doing that. Otherwise you just feel sad. After several years in exile, I finally got the inspiration to go to Medjugorje. It was actually a gift from my husband for my fortieth birthday. I had tried to go once before, but circumstances prevented the trip and I understood it was not God's will. Finally, though, it was time and my eldest daughter and I found ourselves in front of St. James Church. It was her second trip to Medjugorje.

I did not expect or consider that I would experience anything out of the ordinary. My daughter, who loved it on her first trip, made many jokes about people looking for miracles. She affectionately calls Medjugorje a carnival for religious people. She also says it is the happiest place on earth. This young woman initially went there as a rebellious fourteen-year-old, who took the opportunity to travel abroad with her aunt. She returned calm and respectful, prompting my husband to say we would send all our teenagers on pilgrimage.

At any rate, we had a beautiful five days. I experienced a spiritual healing on the mountain. My daughter rested and prayed. A quiet but significant thing happened to me. During my Communions, I spoke with Jesus conversationally. I thought this was beautiful, but it had happened before on occasion so I was not stunned or overcome. I remember telling others that Communions in Medjugorje were powerful. I came home, deeply grateful to Our Lady for bringing us there.

The conversations continued all that winter. At some time in the six months that followed our trip, the conversations leaked into my life and came at odd times throughout the day. Jesus began to direct me with decision and I found it more and more difficult to refuse when He asked me to do this or that. I told no one.

During this time, I also began to experience direction from the Blessed Mother. Their voices are not hard to distinguish. I do not hear them in an auditory way, but in my soul or mind. By this time I knew that something remarkable was occurring and Jesus was telling me that He had special work for me, over and above my primary vocation as wife and mother. He told me to write the messages down and that He would arrange to have them published and disseminated. Looking back, it took Him a long time to get me comfortable enough where I was willing to trust Him. I trust His voice now and will continue to do my best to serve Him, given my constant struggle with weaknesses, faults, and the pull of the world.

Please pray for me as I continue to try to serve Jesus. Please answer "yes" to Him because He so badly needs us and He is so kind. He will take you right into His heart if you let Him. I am praying for you and am so grateful to God that He has given you these words. Anyone who knows Him must fall in love with Him, such is His goodness. If you have been struggling, this is your answer. He is coming to you in a special way through these words and the graces that flow through them.

Please do not fall into the trap of thinking that He cannot possibly mean for you to reach high levels of holiness. As I say somewhere in my writings, the greatest sign of the times is Jesus having to make do with the likes of me as His secretary. I consider myself the B-team, dear friends. Join me and together we will do our little bit for Him.

Message received from Jesus immediately following my writing of the above biographical information:

You see, My child, that you and I have been together for a long time. I was working quietly in your life for years before you began this work. Anne, how I love you. You can look back through your life and see so many "yes" answers to Me. Does that not please you and make you glad? You began to say "yes" to Me long before you experienced extraordinary graces. If you had not, My dearest, I could never have given you the graces or assigned this mission to you. Do you see how important it was that you got up every day, in your ordinary life, and said "yes" to your God, despite difficulty, temptation, and hardship? You could not see the big plan as I saw it. You had to rely on your faith. Anne, I tell you today, it is still that way. You cannot see My plan, which is bigger than your human mind can accept. Please continue to rely on your faith as it brings Me such glory. Look at how much I have been able to do with you, simply because you made a quiet and humble decision for Me. Make another quiet and humble decision on this day and every day, saying, "I will serve God." Last night you served Me by bringing comfort to a soul in pain. You decided against yourself and for Me, through your service to him. There was gladness in heaven, Anne. You are Mine. I am yours. Stay with Me, My child. Stay with Me.

Part One

Spiritual Warfare

Prayer to St. Michael the Archangel

Saint Michael the Archangel, defend us in battle. Be our defense against the wickedness and snares of the devil. May God rebuke him, we humbly pray and do thou, O Prince of the Heavenly Host, by the power of God, cast into hell satan and all the evil spirits who prowl throughout the world seeking the ruin of souls. Amen.

Allegiance Prayer

Dear God in heaven, I pledge my allegiance to You. I give You my life, my work and my heart. In turn, give me the grace of obeying Your every direction to the fullest possible extent. Amen.

Spiritual Warfare

We must accept that the enemy of God is present in any place on earth where he thinks he can lure souls to hell and destroy God's plan. A person who denies the reality of satan is foolish, after all, and will be handicapped in his struggle for unity with God.

God is love, first, foremost, and always. Heaven is all about love and is brimming over and filled with love. Hell is the opposite, the antithesis of heaven. In hell souls will find no love, only hatred.

If God's Kingdom is all about love, then love is the most important thing we need to consider. Perhaps then, if this work is to be of any merit to souls, it should begin with an examination of authentic love and seek to expose fake love.

Where the enemy is present, one can look for a lack of authentic love, which can be partially characterized by a willingness to sacrifice. Real love, which originates in God, willingly accepts that sacrifice and giving are necessary. The enemy's version features selfishness. Clearly we draw a distinction between the love of an infant or child and the love of an adult.

We must examine the relationships around us, most importantly, our own. The enemy will seek to destroy what is good in a relationship and replace it with exploitation and manipulation. As lay apostles, we must look into each relationship in our lives and be certain that we follow Godly principles. We must seek to be genuinely giving, with an awareness that we should strive to set an example of Christ-like behavior to each other.

The devil does not want this, of course. The devil wants to

use us to exploit those around us. People cooperate by using others, perhaps for sex, for money, for power, or ego. We must be scrupulous not to fall into these traps. There is no benefit to reading, or indeed writing a work such as this if we use it only to identify the flaws of others. We must search tirelessly for our own flaws, using the example set by Jesus Christ as our behavioral goal.

How does the devil seek to poison relationships?

The devil sometimes whispers that a person is weak or foolish and tries to inspire us to manipulate that person.

The devil tries to fill us with insecurity, telling us that others take advantage of us and treat us badly.

The devil attempts to persuade us that people do not admire us enough and that people do not see all of our good qualities and efforts.

The devil tries to persuade us that we are misused, unloved, and under-appreciated.

The devil says that we are wasting our time in loving people who are unworthy of our love.

Surely the enemy made similar statements to Jesus.

Such whispering! It never ends, my friends. Be assured that if we are trying to serve our God, we have an enemy who is equally committed to pulling us from our path and drawing us to a path that leads in the opposite direction. There is, after all, a constant battle being waged for our souls.

We are well able for this battle if we are properly armed. The difficulty in today's world is that the devil is like the snake that changes its look based on the environment in which it finds itself. Souls have forgotten the need for allegiance to God. The enemy, emboldened, hides by standing in the open.

This is the most arrogant and defiant type of rebelliousness and the devil mocks God without cease in this way. Of course God is well accustomed to the mockery of the enemy and correctly sees it as meaningless. We must try to follow that example. But many of God's children have wandered further and further away from truth and the enemy is making fools of them.

We must accept that God's enemy wants only our destruction. The enemy of God has an agenda for us that includes unhappiness and eternal despair. The enemy sends temptation. When a person falls prey to a temptation and commits a sin or even merely an action that pulls the soul from goodness, the enemy exults. The enemy mocks humanity and works tirelessly to sow seeds of restlessness and anger, frustration and bitterness.

All people should understand that just as God loves, the devil hates.

This is not complex, for all the enemy tries to cloud this battle in confusion and modern theory. It is simple. The devil hates God's children. We are all God's children. The devil hates us.

God's enemy is our enemy and seeks only our destruction.

As I said, the enemy hides by standing in the open like the well-camouflaged snake. The devil has so well camouflaged himself that we lose sight of him if we are not looking carefully. He blends in. How does he do this? I will tell you. *The enemy calls himself good and dares God's children to state otherwise.*

> "He was a murderer from the beginning, not holding to the truth, for there is no truth in him. When he lies, he speaks his native language, for he is a liar and the father of lies." (*John* 8:44)

The devil arranges for the murder of God's children and calls it choice. Anyone who objects is roared at and accused of being judgmental or against liberty. People are sluggish because they do not pray, and thereby do not fuel their souls with heavenly courage and the light that is truth. It is often easier to sleep on than to become alert and confront the necessity for battle. Which of us will deny that moral courage and a decision to expose the truth is often accompanied by shaking knees? My goodness, how the enemy seeks to intimidate us.

Because many people have drifted away from a position of moral courage, those who retain or choose that position often stand in small numbers. This makes it more difficult, of course, but also more necessary, than if we stood with a majority.

The enemy, always jealous of God, tries to mimic Him. Mimicry is another strategy used by the enemy wherein the devil acts like God by pretending to care about people and by stating that evil principles are really good and merciful to humanity. The devil's language sometimes drips with mercy and compassion and sounds somewhat similar to God's language. Look beyond the language, dear friends.

For example, "choice" sounds like a good and compassionate thing but there is a dead baby at the other end of it.

Mimicry is different from camouflage because camouflage refers to the attempt to resemble an object in appearance. The snake can look like rocks and grass if it is perfectly still. But when the snake acts, or is acted upon, the snake can no longer resemble the rocks and grasses in which it hides. The snake cannot act like rocks and grass because the snake is not, in its nature, a rock or a blade of grass.

I am saying that when the devil is put to the test, the devil can try to hide or mimic God all he wants but he can never be successful because where God is mercy the devil is condemnation.

In the last fifty years we have seen an outcry against poor treatment of women. The outcry, predictably, came from women. This was necessary because women should not be mistreated. I believe it was good and based on truth.

While women began to work for protection and fair treatment, the enemy began to work to distort their goals, whispering that women should not have to be hampered by their duties. This logic was flawed and encouraged women to act against their very nature, a nature that was designed by our heavenly Father to help them and others gain a blessed eternity.

Many women turned against men. Lucifer's plan was shrewd and cunning. A house divided will not stand.

To look at it from another angle, this same time period introduced birth control. What is the truth? The truth is that it can be a bad thing for a woman to have too many pregnancies, too close together. A woman and family can be overwhelmed. It is far better if pregnancies are reasonably spaced. The women's movement, recognizing this, began to reveal it as a difficulty for women. The Church's position agrees and recommends spacing pregnancies. There is one excellent way to space pregnancies and of course that is by limiting sex to times when a woman is unlikely to get pregnant. It's called Natural Family Planning and it is perfectly safe, scientific, and consistent with God's goals for our marriages and families.

Instead of proceeding with God in this matter, the women's movement fell into step with His enemy and birth control was touted as the best protection for women. Protection indeed! Birth control made it possible for women to be treated as objects with far more efficiency and with far fewer immediate consequences. Both men and women are now told that sinful sexual behavior is allowable and acceptable. God's parameters are mocked and ignored. The enemy stands in the open, laughing.

People have been persuaded that they are entitled to have sex when they choose, rejecting any unwanted life that results. Sexual intercourse, by its nature and intent, is a potentially life-giving act. This is God's version.

The enemy's version is that sex can be closed to life and used for physical pleasure only. The enemy's version of sex is selfish, emotionally dangerous, and bad for humanity. The enemy has successfully tempted humanity to distort God's beautiful plan for our sexuality.

God's plan being what it is, life often results from sex. The enemy offers an answer for this, too, and leads souls to avoid consequences by offering widespread contraception and abortion. The devil tells souls that disobedient sex is our business because we are not hurting anyone. Well over 40 million slaughtered babies in the United States alone will one day testify to the lie of that statement.

The problem with the choice argument, which states that a woman should be able to choose what to do with her own body, is that it is not her body that is being destroyed. The little body being destroyed does not belong to her. It is her child's body and this child is a member of the Kingdom of God, sharing the God-given right to life. God uses the mother's womb to protect the child until the child is ready to be born. Women cooperate with God in the process of life. The fact that mothers are offering their infants must leave us dumbfounded at the success of the enemy's campaign in this matter, because many good women have fallen into this trap.

The devil accepts these murders with the greatest glee and

laughter, offering the bodies of these martyrs to our God as evidence of His plan gone wrong. The enemy tells God that we, who were created to develop in the image and likeness of God, have developed into the image and likeness of God's enemy instead.

Imagine God's pain.

Let political leaders and all Christians be warned. You cannot be friends with Jesus Christ and accept abortion. The truth will emerge and each soul will be accountable.

What is the effect of all of this on men? Their sexuality has become terrifically distorted with the most dreadful consequences. The lines of their duty are blurred and the God-given obligation to govern their sexuality has been all but taken away from them. Many are confused and depressed and view women through a prism that highlights only women's sexuality. There is no dignity for men in the plan of the enemy.

Indeed, people are showered with images of sexuality. These images are of women who seduce, of course, because the media seldom offer images of appropriate sexuality.

What is God's plan? God intends that a man and woman enter into a blessed union and then share their sexuality with each other. When God ordains, He blesses the union with a child, who is protected by the parents as the child learns to develop in the image and likeness of God.

The opposite plan, designed by God's enemy, is that people misuse their sexuality, using others for selfish purposes. Modern society wades through the carnage and debris left by the enemy's version. We have broken families, single parent families, rejected babies, people suffering from dreadful diseases, and a veritable sea of individuals who live separated from God and His plan for them. People, confused and sad, look for the source of their pain.

The enemy points to God saying, "God is too demanding of you. God is unreasonable. If we distributed more condoms we would not have disease or the need to abort babies. It is really God's fault because God's Church is against condoms."

One could write a whole book on the ridiculousness of the condom phenomenon in this world. One would think that the condom was the cure for every ill ever confronted by mankind. Our young people must be told that condoms do not always prevent pregnancy and protect against sexually transmitted diseases and that no condom in the world will shield a person from a broken heart and a wounded soul.

The most ludicrous example of the pot calling the kettle black must be the contention by one particular group that the Catholic Church is responsible for the spread of AIDS because the Church does not endorse the use of condoms. We all know how AIDS is spread and it is not through following the teachings of the Catholic Church. We must, if nothing else, note the audacity of that spin.

The truth is that the most successful AIDS prevention program of any in the world was launched in Uganda, where the infection rate declined from about 15% to 5%. Beginning in the 1980s, the Ugandan government worked closely with community and faith-based organizations. The program discouraged high risk sexual behaviors and highlighted education. It is stated that abstinence and marital fidelity appeared to be the most important factors in preventing the spread of HIV/AIDS. This approach also taught, as a last resort, that if a decision was made to engage in high risk sex, a condom was advisable, but generally, the campaign changed behaviors through education and truth. I like the fact that it identified casual sex as high risk. This is telling the truth.

Everything points to sex during this time. The devil distracts us with sex and keeps us looking in the direction of sex. He does this so that we do not look at the truth, which is that we are supposed to be advancing in holiness and helping God to work with others. Sadly, our youth are taught to scorn virtue. The enemy encourages them to acquire wealth and possessions. Imagine the disappointment of the one who dies and meets God when his purpose in life was to acquire material wealth.

A missionary in an underdeveloped part of the world recently contacted us looking for prayers. His congregation was being denied food and water because they were Christians. In this time of famine and drought, many were dying. He ministered to them in their pain. I am sure Jesus flows through this man freely to His starving children. I am also sure that while their bodies are starving, their souls are being nourished in abundance, thanks in part to this lovely member of our family who willingly denies himself to serve them.

The point I am making is that our children need to be told that in many areas of the world there is no food or water. In many areas of the world people are choosing to die for the sake of following Jesus Christ. Children in the West are simply being asked to control their sexual urges.

If we don't educate our youth on chastity, we clearly haven't a hope of getting them to give their lives to the Kingdom as missionaries or religious.

The issue, I believe, is partially one of expectation. The bar of behavior needs to be raised back up to a standard that provides spiritual safety for our youth. The devil's plan for our children must be exposed.

God's plan for us on earth is that we look for Him in every experience. I feel certain that God intends that each person on earth be fed during this time. Western society has been blessed abundantly. God's view of food is that it is a necessity that should be limited to what one needs to fuel the body, but in the West today, food is often viewed as a sensual experience. People are tempted to gluttonous behavior in their treatment of both food and drink. There is a misuse and distortion of food intake. Like sex, souls believe that they are entitled to exactly the type of food they want, whenever they want, and in quantities of their choice.

It would benefit us all to remember that the rest of the world does not live this way. As stated, God's children in other parts of the world are starving. If we consumed less, we could share more. Many people do share and many answer God's call to work with the hungry and needy. This is as it should be and this is good. But if you look at the devil's handiwork in this matter, you will see that many people in the West are sickening themselves through food. What was good has turned bad because it is being abused and misused. The enemy tempts God's children with food that tastes good but is not nutritious. Food items once considered treats have become staples.

The devil encourages us to deny our bodies nothing and we are exhausted from responding to every craving and impulse. Note the shrewdness of this distraction. If we are kept busy by our bodies, dear friends, we forget to nourish our souls and we do not thrive spiritually or physically. We must bring our bodies into submission by telling our bodies "NO." Free of bodily slavery, we will see our souls gain strength and courage.

Another offering by God's enemy is alcohol. Alcohol, taken in moderation, is a good thing. Presumably, Jesus

Himself drank wine.

The enemy has taken the moderate use of alcohol and tempted people to abuse this drug to a level that renders them useless to heaven and dangerous to themselves and others. The devil calls this relaxing and tells people they have a right to relax in this way. The devil says that those who object to this are rigid and lack the ability to have fun. The devil says that this is all innocent and that a person is not harming anyone so he should be free to consume as much alcohol as he chooses.

Dear friends of heaven, reject this. The devil has no shorter, crueler or tighter leash for a person than to lure him into addiction to alcohol or drugs. The devil has mocked me in the past by telling me that he can use those with addictions to work against God's children. He likened these to hand puppets and said that when he cannot make headway with a holy person because of that person's obedience, he consoles himself by toying with those whom he influences through addiction. We must not subject ourselves to this slavery. Freedom from addiction is available to us and God wants us to be free. Our Lady beseeches us to become free.

Which one of us has the strength to walk away from an addiction? Certainly I did not. God had to do it for me so that I could be free of a nicotine addiction. He will do it for each one of us, but we have to have the courage to take the first step and decide to at least try to be liberated.

Many people use alcohol to numb emotional pain. This self-medicating strategy has the potential to turn into a physical and psychological dependence.

We must treat all substances, food, alcohol, and drugs, with the greatest awareness that just as heaven has a plan for the use of these things, the devil has a plan for the misuse of them.

Prayer

In the past, prayer was considered part of life for Catholics. God's plan is that we work and live in union and communion with Him. In this way, He can be part of our daily life. Daily living, taken with Christ, offers continual opportunity for growth in virtue and holiness. Families praying together provide an atmosphere of goodness and morality for their children. God is generous to those who proceed in this way and children feel safe and valued.

The enemy persuades us that prayer is of no value. Often the enemy has lured us into such a state of busyness that we believe we do not have time to pray. Brothers and sisters, how could this be God's plan? Clearly this frenzy of busyness and noise is not an offering from heaven. Just as God wishes us to proceed calmly and methodically through our daily lives, the enemy whips us into a frenzy of activity. There is constant distraction through music, noise, talking, bickering, and endless discussion.

Why has the enemy targeted prayer? Let us consider what prayer accomplishes. At the very least, in my life, prayer grants me the grace to take the enemy's version of reality and replace it with God's truth.

The enemy tells me I am a failure. God tells me I am succeeding because I am choosing my vocation over my own desires. The enemy tells me to quit this mission, for countless reasons. God tells me to continue on in His will. The enemy tells me God does not care about my pain. God tells me that He cares deeply and perfectly about any pain I suffer and that He sees my pain as valuable and temporary and that He will bring great things from it.

The enemy tells me that the world is a disaster. God tells

me that He has a plan and that the world will come right.

The enemy brings distress. God brings peace.

The enemy offers a distorted and dangerous version of God's plan and often it is only through prayer that we can identify the traps and inconsistencies offered by the devil. We need the Sacraments, as well as constant acts of love and obedience. Time with Christ, time in prayer, moves us AWAY from the reach of the enemy.

Prayer brings peace. Prayer brings gentleness. Prayer brings resolution between warring parties. Prayer brings Christ into the world and sits Him at every table. Prayer brings truth and justice and joy.

If we find ourselves too busy for prayer, then we are altogether too busy.

Spiritual warfare is often ignored by clergy in that the subject is not addressed from the pulpit with any regularity. It is true that the world glorifies God's enemy and we do not wish to contribute to that mistake. Additionally, there is a need to steer people away from superstition. This is important. At the same time, to pretend that the enemy does not exist is to disarm a population of Christians who are under relentless assault but who think they are doing just fine.

We need to increase the awareness that a battle is being waged. People should be warned that if they are not willing to fight, they will have to be willing to accept defeat because the spiritual walk is not one where it is possible to stand still. One way or the other, we are moving. If we are not moving closer to Christ, the chances are excellent that we are moving away from Him.

Thoughts

To be alert in spiritual warfare means to be constantly examining the source of our thoughts.

For example, does Jesus tell us that our cross is too heavy and we should drop it on someone else or abandon it?

Does Jesus tell us that life is unfair to us and we should blame others?

Does Jesus continually remind us how badly we have been treated, inspiring us to bitterness?

Obviously, these are not the inspirations that come from the Savior. Instead, Jesus tells us that our cross, however heavy, is manageable if we carry it with His help. He tells us that life on earth is not always fair, it is true, but that perfect justice awaits us in heaven. Jesus asks that we forgive others and be at peace with the flaws of those around us. That is the way Jesus talks.

We must learn to listen closely to our thoughts and be on guard, always judging who is inspiring us. We should get into the habit of conforming our thoughts to Christ's thoughts. In this way we will be granted the peace that eludes followers of the world.

This is spiritual warfare and I believe it begins with our thoughts. Let us look even more closely and examine the war in terms of individual battles.

Never in our walk is it more important to trust God than when one is in the middle of a spiritual battle. Even the most seasoned apostle can suddenly find himself tumbling about in the grip of something that feels a bit like being a gym shoe in a clothes dryer. Such pain and confusion! This should be our first clue, of course, that we are being targeted.

A fellow apostle once said, "It's no problem once you know it's the devil. But usually someone else has to tell you that."

How true. Who would fail to pick up a sword if someone approached them and began to duel? The enemy is more clever than that, though. The enemy comes in the form of a hurtful comment from a friend, an overdrawn bank account, a misunderstanding where our words are twisted and thrown back at us in mockery.

The enemy can come dressed in perfect logic, with a superior attitude and a patronizing smile offering some "good advice."

Much of what we are asked to do as lay apostles will not make sense when measured against the world's standards of what is right and wrong, wise or unwise. We will sometimes appear foolish if we work for heaven, particularly in the eyes of those who work for heaven but do so safely within the limits of worldly acceptance.

We must always identify the author of the thoughts. My friends, the more we love God and the more we are asked to work for God, the more committed we must be to conversation with God. This is a given but it bears constant repeating because while in the midst of a spiritual battle, we find that we tend to avoid prayer. This adds to the confusion, of course, and is like wearing hiking boots to run. You'll move more comfortably through the attack if you pray. This is yet another reason why firm spiritual habits are a must.

How It Feels to be Under Attack

How do we know when we are being attacked? I will speak first for myself and, with God's help, light will be shed on this elusive concept.

When I am being attacked I feel upset. I feel anxious or hurt. My thoughts are unruly and what formerly seemed comfortable and right seems unsafe and frightening. I sometimes feel as though I am underwater and cannot find the surface. What formerly was up now seems down, or sidewise, or gone altogether. I feel as though I cannot get my bearings. I feel angry at times and rebellious. I must use the word outraged as when I feel outraged, I know I'm in trouble. The doubts that I have when under attack are something to behold. Following are some thoughts consistent with resistance:

> I'm not putting up with this.
>
> This is too much to ask.
>
> I'm quitting this work and I mean it this time.
>
> I'm not making peace with that person. I'm just not.
>
> How dare this person behave this way?
>
> I'm never talking to that person again.
>
> It's not fair, Lord. It's just not fair.
>
> What is God thinking giving me a job like He has given me?
>
> I'm not holy enough for this.
>
> I'm not up for this.

God has overestimated my capacity for
   humiliation.

I've messed it all up. I'm heaven's worst enemy.

Jesus can't stand me. He's just too nice to say so.

I'm worthless to Christ.

We won't have enough money.

Nothing is going well. It's all a disaster.

Let's take the concept of money, as the enemy can play
gleefully with our lack of trust in God's providence. When I
begin to worry over how I will manage in five years time, a
little red light begins to blink in my head. God provides for
the birds of the air. The odds are good that if He wants our
families cared for, He will arrange for their care. It is better
to say, "Do we have a food or shelter emergency today? At
this moment?" If not, then we should probably trust Him
and get on with His work.

It insults Jesus to show so little trust in Him and yet we all
fail at times in this regard. God's enemy will take our hand
and walk with us down this path by planting thoughts of
impending disaster for our missions and loved ones.

Clearly, it helps to continue on a path of separating needs
from wants. If we separate our needs from our wants, the
enemy's power will diminish and the Lord will have apostles
who understand that He provides what we require.

In times where we do not have what we need, such as
occurs in emergency situations, we must wait peacefully for
the Lord to send help, offering our sacrifice up to Him.
There are some people who lack basic necessities such as
food and water. The Lord wants us to remember that even
in this, the worst case scenario from a human standpoint,

we will eventually lie down to die and He will come for us.

I remember being told years ago that I would require medication for the rest of my life. I became very depressed over this. My father did not understand my distress. I spoke to him in frustration and said, "Don't you understand? I need this to live. What will happen if I'm marooned on an island and I don't have it?"

He said, "You'll die."

I burst out laughing. It was then that I discovered that I am not afraid to die.

Another way I know I'm being attacked is when little things stack up against me and everything seems to go wrong. Contentious phone calls, ugly emails, children breaking religious statues and fighting, computer freezing, files lost, printer jammed, keys missing, car broken down, cashier throwing money at me . . . and all in the half-hour before a meeting where God's interests are being furthered. Who has not had a day like this? Add to the experience some feelings of confusion, fear, anger and a hint of anxiety.

It is often at this point that I understand the company I am in. I then focus completely on the job at hand, talking to Jesus as I proceed. I remind Him that this is His work and that while I am willing, I am struggling. I make myself get very, very calm.

Once, before an important meeting, all of the above occurred and the house filled with a mysterious stench. My husband literally walked me to the car and said, "Go." I did, without my purse and the documents I intended to bring. I had to take his car because my tire was low on air, my keys had disappeared, and I could not find my purse.

We behave differently when we are attacked, depending on both our personalities and the nature of the attack. Some people get tearful, some angry, some frustrated or confused, some irritable, some depressed and quiet, some loud and aggressive.

There is a temptation to respond in kind when someone comes at us aggressively or in an argumentative or confrontational manner. Please resist this temptation. All of heaven rejoices when we resist the temptation to further the enemy's plans. We must struggle heroically against the temptation to judge the one attacking us. If we respond like the Lamb, with the example Jesus has set for us, the enemy's ugly plan will lay in shreds at his feet.

Yes, we must strive to treat others as Jesus would, most particularly when they hurt us. If we view our attacker with compassion, we will be correctly identifying the true enemy.

> "For we wrestle not against flesh and blood, but against principalities, against powers, against the rulers of the darkness of this world, against spiritual wickedness in high places." *Ephesians* 6:12

It will help to look beyond the one who attacks us to the possible author of that person's thoughts. Anger, while inevitable at times, can be a waste of energy. We must save our strength and direct it to serving God and allowing His Kingdom to come through us on every single day.

When we identify symptoms of the devil's anger or resistance, it helps to ask the following question:

What is it that the enemy seeks to spoil?

Quite often the answer will be peace, be it peace in the home, the workplace, or the world at large. Or the enemy could seek to destroy a relationship that is necessary for God's plan to advance. Remember that the enemy is the destroyer of peace. We must always work to establish and maintain peace.

I try to look at situations in two ways. I consider first, what is it that the enemy would like me to do? How is the devil setting me up? Then I consider what decision or response would please Jesus most. What does Jesus want me to do? Therein lay both the struggle and the opportunity for holiness. The soul groans. Humanity objects. Growth pains are evident. There are times when we say, "Lord, it's too hard." At times we fail. But if we can learn to identify and distinguish between the Lord's way and the enemy's way, we are at least in the game.

We must be prepared for battle by being smaller, meeker, and more humble than God's enemy. Our Leader was meek and humble of heart, after all. Forgiveness was a way of life for Jesus. He remained calm, even when falsely arrested. It is He whom we seek to follow.

I experienced a rather fierce period of resistance this morning. I was not surprised, given my assignment for the day. I was feeling determination but it was an angry determination. I took this to Christ and said, "Lord, I can't write this piece angrily. I need to be humble and calm. Please calm my soul, Lord, and make me small and quiet." He did, of course.

In this mission, our motto is **make it smaller**. For example, if someone criticizes the mission, we determine whether or not the criticism has foundation. If it does, we apologize and try to fix the problem. If it does not, we get on with the job at hand.

If the attack is from the devil, it will usually be a storm in a teacup but whatever the problem, we do not give it too much attention. We deal with it as best we can and then get on with the Lord's work. The enemy wants to fan the flames of these upsets, causing all manner of distraction. This is important. If we are all talking and sputtering about what this one said about that one, we are not praising God and helping God to save souls.

The enemy seeks to distract us. The enemy baits us. We must refuse to take the bait. Peace in everything. We must not be distracted from holiness, from our duties and from God's work.

I am careful never to be too impressed by the enemy's paltry power. The enemy shouts and roars, blows and bellows, but it is the empty raging of one with no real strength. Those with real power speak softly. They do not need to yell.

Remember that if Jesus Christ is bigger than the Empire State Building, in terms of power and strength and influence, the devil is, in comparison, the size and strength of a little stinging ant. He can sting but he cannot topple the Empire State Building. As I have said in the past, let's not gather around the stinging ant, admiring his power when we stand in the shadow of the Empire State Building. We must turn around and face the Almighty, admiring and relying on His limitless power.

Jesus reminded me of this one morning. I was concerned about a dreadfully unjust and false attack. I felt at a loss to respond. Jesus said, ***"Anne, I conquered the world. I can handle this."***

During periods of duress, it is important that we be very gentle with ourselves. We must not condemn ourselves or judge ourselves more harshly than the Lord judges us. The enemy delights when we think, poor me. I'm not holy enough. Surely the Lord should cast me out of the family. Surely the Lord can do without the service of one who fails as I have just failed.

We will all fail. We will at times lose patience with others. We will also, at times, mistakenly take the bait from the enemy and be drawn into upset and disorder. There are times when we will be the cause of the upset and disorder. But to beat ourselves up over failures is to prolong the enemy's influence. Jesus has no need of perfect apostles or He would have created some. He needs us, in all of our imperfection. And He needs us to be humble so we must rejoice when we experience our humanity.

If nothing else, mistakes remind us that Christ is King and we are not.

Remember, too, that Jesus allows attacks. The devil has no power that Christ does not allow him. Jesus allows us to experience spiritual warfare so that we can grow in holiness and trust.

With regard to spiritual warfare, my spiritual director often says, "Expect it. Count on it. See it coming."

We must expect resistance and become adept at weathering storms. It is terrifically helpful to have humility. Ask God for humility each day as without it you will be vulnerable.

It is a standing joke in our family that a request to heaven for humility is usually answered within minutes. If you lack humility, my friends, you will inevitably land on your backside. In fairness, we all land like that at times. Our humanity guarantees it. Be assured, though, that a lack of humility insures a far more painful landing.

Given the goal of exposing the enemy and the attacks of the enemy, I asked some friends to describe spiritual warfare and how they felt when they were being attacked. Following are some of the responses from committed and experienced apostles.

A priest: "I become uninterested in God's work. I have no desire for it. In fact, it's an annoyance. I feel depressed, angry, and irritable. I feel a desire to withdraw from people, or even talk to people. I have no desire to pray. I feel fear about the future and a sense of complete inadequacy. My self esteem dips. I feel no desire to pray, but eventually I experience a hunger, as though I hadn't been fed in days. I know this to be the need for Christ."

A mother: "I feel like I am an ineffective parent. I feel I'm a lousy mother and that all of my children are doing badly. I feel as though everyone is against me, and should be more helpful to me. I feel like no matter how hard I try, I cannot pull it all together. I am certain there is no hope of turning my troubles around. I think, this is just too hard. Please Lord, take me now. I know that God allows this so that I'll learn to trust Him. But while I am in it, I am sometimes angry that heaven is not helping me enough! I have found myself in a car yelling at heaven, 'Where are you all?!' "

A father: "The devil wants us to be silent about these things so he can corner people and make them think they are alone. He does not want the Light of Christ brought to the person, but rather wants to keep him in his darkness. He is the deceiver. Fr. Corapi says the devil's favorite color is gray. He wants confusion and disorder, and a literal blurring of what is light and darkness, truth and lies, right and wrong. When I am being attacked, I feel a sense of uneasiness and even fatigue physically. I have thoughts that my contribution is worthless and a waste of time. I lose clarity about what I am doing and why I am doing it. I eventually figure it out, but it takes time. Many times, it is something my wife says that makes me recognize that it is happening. She brings me clarity when I am clouded by these thoughts.The way I work out of the confusion is to ask Our Lady for help. I pray a Rosary and the darkness quickly leaves. It is often a tough task to even start the Rosary, as there is usually some resistance. Many times I will leave the house or office and pray while walking. Once I begin concentrating on the prayers and the mysteries, it quickly passes."

A father: "I used to think that resistance, or the obstacles placed in our way by the forces of darkness, did not really affect me all that much. After all, who am I? Certainly not one worthy of the devil's attention. Why create problems for me when there are much bigger fish to fry? Why not go hassle a saint …or trip up a priest or religious…or make the day really ugly for someone already at heaven's door?

"The devil doesn't really bother with run-of-the-mill souls like me, does he?

"Then, after much reading and meditation, I realized I was a good example of where the devil was being especially successful. He had upset my plans, kept me away from due attention to my spiritual life, and was constantly slowing or even stopping my climb up the mountain of holiness. I never had a clue. I was so busy worrying about the tigers closest to my throat—the mortgage check that was due, the problems besetting my adult children, criticism and harsh words from 'friends'—that I paid more attention to the symptoms than to the cause.

"This was exactly what the evil one wanted me to think. In doing so, all my energies were diverted into 'coping with life' when instead I should have been concentrating upon 'coping with evil.' But how was I to combat all these obstacles coming up in my life? How was I to turn these diversions to good?

"Suddenly the answer was before me. I took the easy way out...I surrendered it all to Jesus. Let life—or evil—do its best to capture my attention, but Jesus will see that I remain on track. I let Him handle the details. If I never lose sight of the top of the mountain, then I will not stumble over all those boulders placed in my path. My Morning Offering prayer to Jesus is my key weapon in overcoming resistance."

A sister: "Spiritual warfare shows in the chaos of all who work with us. Office problems that do not exist in our office show up right on schedule before an important date for ministry work."

A priest: "I know the struggle is on when I feel like a weak link."

A mother: "Without any hesitation, I can say that a spiritual attack takes away the desire to be with God. When I'm not under attack, I long for Him and for Adoration time. Under attack, I have to fight against myself to get there, even though it's the one place I most need to be. Same for prayer. I pray virtually all day long most times, in one form or another. Under attack I have to literally force myself to pray. That's when I draw on the words of Scripture that state that we should always pray and never lose heart even when we don't feel like it or want to; otherwise I'd convince myself my prayers were worthless because my heart wasn't in them. This has surprised me in the past since I thought I would cry out to God in trouble and ignore Him in good times. My reality is the opposite. Only now do I recognize this as the insidious attack that it is. Does this make sense? Even the discussion of it is confusing. I have a temptation to stay in bed instead of getting up for daily Mass because my body hurts a lot. It is a one member pity party. I have a temptation to give in to my fears. Those attacks are the most terrible. This honesty is painful but it's the truth so why not?

"Most people, I think, aren't even familiar with the concept of spiritual warfare. It's an advanced term introduced only when you start your climb up the mountain. Then, even before learning the term, you meet the force of it big-time. After that, it becomes all too familiar to you and a partner for as long as you climb. It would be good to alert the reader to the power in calling on the NAME OF JESUS. It may be the ultimate tool in the battle."

Young apostle: "I get crabby. Really crabby. And tired."

A priest: "Spiritual warfare is a given. We have to assume opposition, both from within and without.

"We're less than perfect, of course. Sometimes we assume we're doing things for very pure motives when in fact our motives are selfish and not at all pure. We suffer from weakness of will and an inclination to evil that is within our nature.

"From the outside, people may laugh at us or ridicule us. This is discouraging. At difficult times one thinks, is it worth continuing? Why the constant battle? Life should be easier than this. At worst I think that surely there is another way to make a living."

A Sister: "I take things personally, focusing in on myself instead of concentrating on what the other person is going through. I feel an uneasiness in my stomach. I feel sad. I want to get off and be alone. It brings home the need to spend more time in prayer."

A priest: "I feel anger and aggression coming at me and I feel down and depressed. I can feel doubt and fear and an uncertainty. I feel very put upon. I also get sick before important work with irritating sicknesses such as colds. A sure fire antidote is to go to Confession. Repentance is the way to beat it."

A father: "How do I know when I am being attacked by the enemy? What does spiritual warfare feel like to me?

"Frankly, I do not usually know when I am being attacked by the enemy. He is smarter than I am. He makes me feel that it is just my human weakness, my human nature that makes me sin, and he has nothing to do with it. He knows that if he makes his presence more apparent, I would then realize the gravity of my sin, and shun both him and sin.

"Indeed our fallen nature tends toward pride, lust, greed and the other deadly sins. If I accept these weaknesses as natural to human flesh, I have already lost half the battle against the enemy. Only in prayer do I realize that I am involved in spiritual battle, and only by the grace and mercy of God do I defend myself with the weapons that He has provided, most specially the Holy Eucharist and the Holy Rosary. Very powerful are the Gifts of the Holy Spirit and living life according to the Beatitudes, Jesus' stairway to heaven. Living in this way, I trust in the mercy of the Lord and the enemy usually leaves me alone.

"But I know I have to be careful not to be complacent. It could be a temptation, not feeling the need of climbing further up the mountain, happy to be where I am, avoiding spiritual warfare. Who really wants to duel with the enemy? He could eliminate me with one stroke. It is better that he leaves me alone. This complacency shows my trust in Jesus is imperfect. If I truly trust Him, I should be ready to go where He leads me, even to the frontlines, in mortal combat with the enemy.

"Jesus, increase my trust in You!"

A mother: "I learned about spiritual warfare as a charismatic. The idea was to come against bad spirits—not just devils per se but say: 'the spirit of depression,' 'the spirit of disgruntlement,' 'the spirit of anxiety.' Anything negative in my consciousness was seen as something to 'work' against rather than to sink into passively."

Following is the description by a priest who is very seasoned in battle. I set his description apart from the others as it is a more detailed response.

> **A priest:** "My experience is that attacks can range from the annoying, through the challenging and difficult, to the frightening."

1. Annoying

    a. These usually are stirred up by working on our emotional wounds, infiltrating them and increasing their strength. When I can spot anger that comes from fear, memory of rejection, etc. that threatens to ruin or weaken a relationship, I either see clearly the work of evil spirits or presume on the basis of memory that there are such spirits at work and I say: 'In the name of Jesus Christ, I renounce the spirit of...' anger, fear, rejection or what ever, and then rely on the Lord to be there to moderate my emotional disorders.

    b. The same rhythm is present in prayer either through distractions or through bogus 'consolations.' St. Ignatius gives some rules for discernment here: If I have any doubts I pray something like 'Holy Spirit come' and look at Jesus. There is a helpful little book that I have just come across: *The Discernment of Spirits* by Timothy M. Gallagher, OMV (New York: Crossroad, 2005).

2. Challenging and Difficult

a. Sometimes annoying attacks can be extremely intense. We have no doubt that we are under attack: fear, hatred, lust, "racing mind" that we cannot shut off. We are called upon to do battle, sometimes feeling a strange torpor and sense of hopelessness. I pray to Our Lady, call upon Jesus, visit the Blessed Sacrament, get prayed over—often it is the first movement of resistance that turns the tide.

   i. *1 Peter* **5:8-10** 8 Be sober and vigilant. Your opponent the devil is prowling around like a roaring lion looking for [someone] to devour. 9 Resist him, steadfast in faith, knowing that your fellow believers throughout the world undergo the same sufferings. 10 The God of all grace who called you to His eternal glory through Christ [Jesus] will Himself restore, confirm, strengthen, and establish you after you have suffered a little.

   ii. *James* **1:12-17** 12 Blessed is the man who perseveres in temptation, for when he has been proved he will receive the crown of life that He promised to those who love Him. 13 No one experiencing temptation should say, "I am being tempted by God"; for God is not subject to temptation to evil, and He

Himself tempts no one. 14 Rather, each person is tempted when he is lured and enticed by his own desire. 15 Then desire conceives and brings forth sin, and when sin reaches maturity it gives birth to death. 16 Do not be deceived, my beloved brothers: 17 all good giving and every perfect gift is from above, coming down from the Father of Lights, with Whom there is no alteration or shadow caused by change.

iii. *James* **4:6-7** 6 But He bestows a greater grace; therefore, it says: 'God resists the proud, but gives grace to the humble.' 7 So submit yourselves to God. Resist the devil, and he will flee from you.

b. The same symptoms appear when there is opposition scheming against what we think God wants. It is intense, little and big things go wrong: we start to speak against the opponents in a public and bitter way; we get discouraged and want to quit. For me, only a long time with the Lord (usually a battle to get started) and the advice of a spiritual director or trusted friend lifts the discouragement, complaining, etc. This kind of attack can go on for a long time, usually with breaks to keep us sane and not fixated on the problem.

3. Frightening

a. **Low grade:** We just want to get out of there and quit whatever we are doing. There is often the message: 'If you start to pray against me,

I'll punish you for it.' This happened often to me in the early days of my time in solitude (4-5 days a week). I just kept praying. When I asked the Lord if I should humble myself and go back to the main house of the community and admit I couldn't handle it, I felt He told me to stay. I know now that this is right.

b. **High grade:** An evil spirit is undoubtedly there and is trying to frighten us and stop us from something. The most dramatic time of this for me was in a semi-solitude cabin—I cried out to the Lord and the demon left. I felt the demon's hatred and his manipulation of my angry 'do-gooder' spirit to drive me to exhaustion and heart attack. I changed a lot of my life after that and began to realize that God had forced that demon to show himself in order to warn me.

There are also attacks against groups, families, communities, etc. These prey on the same weaknesses mentioned above: fear, old rejections, jealousy, etc., but they direct the animosity to others. We look for those who 'agree' and divide the group. There are spirits who lead some to form a clique and criticize others, stirring up animosity; there are spirits who work on our emotions so that what one person says is heard in a twisted manner by another. The remedies are first: humility, humility and humility. Then, a genuine effort toward love and reconciliation—the more quickly this is done, the more likely there will be success. Then mutual prayer and cleansing of the environment with prayer and the sacramentals: holy water, holy oil, etc. Never wait for the other person to begin. Accept the suffering of risking the first step. Count on the Lord and pray. Get help when needed and then continue to pray prayers of protection, especially to St. Michael. Evil spirits cannot stay long in an atmosphere of humility and love.

There are also attacks against whole nations and civilizations: Nazism is an example. All the attacks on the dignity of married love is another. This takes place through a gradual hardening of heart and darkening of the mind. Overthrowing this kind of darkness is the work of Jesus and Mary with their army. The first protection and counter-attack is obedience to the Catholic Church; then deep prayer for converted theologians who can be brought through purification to be mystics. The darkness facing the Church now began to be formed by Satan in the 14th century. He wants to destroy humanity. The best way is to destroy the family. The best way to destroy the family is to confuse men and women regarding God's plan for marriage and family and his will for the place of sexuality. Here our contribution is a genuine chastity and incessant prayer for the Church, the bulwark of truth.

Philippians 2:1-16

1 If there is any encouragement in Christ, any solace in love, any participation in the Spirit, any compassion and mercy, 2 complete my joy by being of the same mind, with the same love, united in heart, thinking one thing. 3 Do nothing out of

selfishness or out of vainglory; rather, humbly regard others as more important than yourselves, 4 each looking out not for his own interests, but (also) everyone for those of others. 5 Have among yourselves the same attitude that is also yours in Christ Jesus, 6 Who, though He was in the form of God, did not regard equality with God something to be grasped. 7 Rather, He emptied Himself, taking the form of a slave, coming in human likeness; and found human in appearance, 8 He humbled Himself, becoming obedient to death, even death on a cross. 9 Because of this, God greatly exalted Him and bestowed on Him the name that is above every name, 10 that at the name of Jesus every knee should bend, of those in heaven and on earth and under the earth, 11 and every tongue confess that Jesus Christ is Lord, to the glory of God the Father. 12 So then, my beloved, obedient as you have always been, not only when I am present but all the more now when I am absent, work out your salvation with fear and trembling. 13 For God is the One Who, for His good purpose, works in you both to desire and to work. 14 Do everything without grumbling or questioning, 15 that you may be blameless and innocent, children of God without blemish in the midst of a crooked and perverse generation, among whom you shine like lights in the world, 16 as you hold on to the word of life, so that my boast for the day of Christ may be that I did not run in vain or labor in vain.

Be Not Afraid

The words of our fellow apostles assure us of two things. One, we are all in the same boat when it comes to spiritual warfare, and two, there are many ways to fight back. Apostles should expect to be confronted with the need for battle and apostles should never be afraid.

The Holy Father, Pope John Paul II, said often, "Be not afraid."

He also said, "On the day of Pentecost, Peter was the first to speak to the gathered Israelites and to others who had travelled various distances. He reminded them of the wrong committed by those who had nailed Christ to the cross, and then he confirmed His Resurrection. He exhorted the people to conversion and to Baptism. Thanks to the work of the Holy Spirit, Christ could have confidence in Peter, He could lean on him—on him and on all the other apostles." (*Crossing the Threshold of Hope, p.9*)

My friends, Jesus allows struggle and difficulty in our lives and in our service to Him because He knows we can take it. He knows we won't quit. He can lean on us. Jesus needs to take His consolation where He can get it, so we must be at peace if He counts us as good friends who will accept a share of the cross with Him and continue to serve.

In my experience, the Lord protects all of the important things. At times the sky darkens so blackly that our vision can be obscured. We can walk in what seems to be darkness at times, but heaven is not dark and our soul is not dark, for all we carry the cross.

Christ conquered the world. We don't have to worry about doing that. We simply have to serve Him quietly in the day in which we find ourselves.

Things to Remember

• **Be calm.** In fact, the greater the resistance, the greater is the necessity for calm. If you are not calm, take some time and get calm. Heaven has difficulty helping an apostle who is excited or angry. I speak from the greatest experience in this case. The enemy can damage God's goals if an apostle allows himself to be drawn into upset.

• **Identify the author of the thought.** Is this thought from heaven? Or is this thought from the enemy of heaven? Jesus told me that this concept is very pleasing to Him.

• **Identify the possible courses of action.** What does the enemy hope I will do? What is it that God needs me to do? What is it that God is asking me to do?

I ask myself, "What would a saint do in this situation?" I personally do not often attain the holiest response, but it is good to identify goals. The closer we move to heaven's objectives in each situation, the further we move from the enemy's objectives. Aim high.

• **Be silent.** During difficulty, spend as much time in silence as possible. Say the Rosary. Adore the Eucharist. Get to Mass. Get to Confession. During a period of difficulty we should bless ourselves with holy water often throughout the day. It helps if we concentrate on being very little, very humble, and staying as quiet as we can.

• **Stay in the present.** If we allow ourselves to be worried about the future, we allow ourselves to be distracted from what God needs in the present. Concentrate on this. Practice. Staying in the present is a habit that liberates an apostle.

• **Seek wise counsel.** Talk to a fellow apostle who exhibits good judgment. We must not speak to someone worldly and expect to get heavenly advice.

• **Praise God.** Find a reason to thank God. At times we may be struggling dreadfully. I know people who carry extraordinarily heavy crosses. But in everything there is room to praise God. Sometimes it might be something as simple as, "Lord, thank You that this car started. Lord, thank You that I have electricity today. Jesus, thank You for any medical care my family receives." Many people have cars that do not start or no cars at all. Many suffer without benefit of any medical care. Sometimes electricity does not work or is unavailable. It could always be worse. Always.

• **Pray.** I say the following over and over. "Jesus I love You. I'm here to serve You. I want what You want, Lord. Don't let me disappoint You, Jesus. I pledge my allegiance to You, Father."

I find that the Allegiance Prayer (see page 3) rights me, as if I remind myself that I have given my life, my work, and my heart to God, it all belongs to Him and any opinion of my own is irrelevant.

• **This will pass.** Whatever it is, it will pass. Eventually the struggle will end and our perspective will come right again. Often the upside down feeling passes from one moment to another so we should be at peace and wait it out.

Who is the Devil?

The FBI uses criminal profiling to assist with crime investigation and prevention. Profiling an offender helps to identify one likely to commit a certain type of crime. It is good to know our enemy because we can then protect ourselves from those who seek to hurt us. Below is a list of characteristics of the devil.

- Arrogant
- Cruel
- Proud
- Hateful
- Envious
- Angry
- Jealous
- Liar
- Cold
- Unfeeling
- Duplicitous
- Callous
- Selfish in the extreme
- Unkind
- Sneaky
- Sly
- Unscrupulous
- Manipulative
- Stubborn
- Hates innocence
- Unfaithful
- Mocking
- Destructive
- Slippery
- Gleeful at humanity's pain
- False, phoney, fake
- Mimics holiness/ goodness/honesty
- Disobedient
- Dishonest
- Evil
- Tricky
- Never changing in terms of his goals
- Always seeking destruction of mankind
- Slave to his hatred, it rules him, dictates his every action and emotion

- Raging, furious
- Did I say arrogant?
- Ultimately helpless, which fuels the rage
- Uses humanity like playthings
- Greedy
- Bullying
- Fair weather friend
- Gluttonous
- Instills fear and confusion
- Aggressive
- Blows hard, rants/raves
- Mixes bad with good to confuse
- Mixes truth with lies to confuse
- Seeks to incite, seduce, disillusion
- Leads away from duty
- Distorts truth and motivation
- Humiliates, destroys dignity and integrity
- Seeks to mould souls into his image as mimicry of God
- Inconsistent in strategies, blends, adapts, changes tactics when necessary

Remember that the devil despises obedience because he is powerless against it. When he approaches a person who is obedient, the devil slams into an impenetrable barrier. This fills him with fury because he is helpless.

The devil can use a guilty conscience powerfully so we must be diligent about accepting God's forgiveness and making the most of the abundant graces dispensed in the Sacrament of Reconciliation.

Consider that God has a gift for each of us in the confessional. This gift has been hand designed by God, who looks deeply into our soul and determines exactly what we need at a particular moment. Nobody knows us like our Savior. Picture this beautiful gift, waiting in the confessional for us. How many leave Christmas gifts unopened under the tree on Christmas morning? Very few, I suspect. And yet, how many of us walk past the Sacrament of Reconciliation without going in and accepting the beautiful gifts the Lord has prepared for us?

Lay apostles pledge to go to Confession monthly. We will benefit immensely from the loyal practice of this pledge.

God's Forgiveness

God offers us forgiveness, regardless of the sins we have committed. God's forgiveness has no strings or limits attached. God's forgiveness does not come and go. God does not make forgiveness available one day and then withdraw the offer of it the next day.

The forgiveness of God is and always will be.

Like everything else about God, His forgiveness is perfect. Once it is given, it will not be taken away. God's forgiveness does not rely on anything in us.

Are you sorry for your sins? If the answer is yes, then you have nothing to worry about. Go to Confession if you are a Catholic and everything will be fine.

Some people recall a bad experience in Confession. They cite this as the reason they no longer go to Confession or indeed pray or go to Mass. This is heartbreaking. Be aware that Jesus calls priests from the group that is humanity. Priests are human. If a priest behaved badly to you, God will deal with him. Be assured that the Lord knows the sins of His priests. We must also be assured that when we die and stand before God, He will not ask us what everyone else did wrong. He will ask us for an account of OUR life. Look past the priest to Jesus Christ. Do not allow a bad experience to pull you away from God's love and from all that He offers through His Church.

It is good for people to understand that there is no limit to God's forgiveness. Some people think that their sins, their malice and the damage they have done to others, makes it impossible for God to forgive them. They feel they will always be permanently excluded from God's family. This is only possible if a person refuses to repent and wishes to be excluded.

Some people think they do not want to go to Confession and confess their past sins because it means they are making a commitment to perfection. They think, I'm not ready to be perfect. I'm not ready to change. I'm not ready to completely give up some of my habits or behaviors.

Please, please, please do not let this stop you from going to Confession. Jesus knows you will fail again. He accepts this. If there is the smallest desire in you to try to do the smallest bit better for God, then you should go to Confession and let Christ, through the priest, help you. Conversion is an ongoing thing. We do not become perfect in a day. We do not even become perfect in a lifetime. But we do need to admit that we can improve and begin to try.

Think small steps and the Lord will do big things.

Do not avoid your role in the renewal because you have sinned. If you are repentant, you are just the type of person needed. One who comes to God in humility can be restored to purity in an instant. God has no difficulty in forgiving a repentant sinner. It is far more difficult for God to deal with a person who serves heaven but takes all the credit. It is God who grants holiness, after all. It is God who performs miracles.

What makes a valuable lay apostle? I must say that God loves humility and willingness. When a person encounters someone who loves God and who is humble, he is drawn to that person and drawn to God. When a person encounters someone who loves God but who is arrogant in his service, he is not drawn to that person and sadly, an opportunity for conversion can be missed.

I have had the smallest experience of both purgatory and heaven. Both places are filled with repentant sinners so we will fit right in, as long as we admit we're not perfect, say we're sorry for our sins and allow God to heal us. God has a short memory when it comes to our mistakes and a long memory when it comes to any cooperation we give to Him.

If I were to meet someone who was concerned about his past sins, I would advise that person to read the section of Volume Four entitled *God Speaks to Sinners*. I would also advise that person to acquaint himself with the mission of St. Faustina and the Chaplet of Divine Mercy. These things will comfort a person.

But there is nothing to worry about because the truth of the matter is simple.

God forgives.

Part Two

Snapshots of Reality

In the following pages, Anne gives small illustrations of spiritual warfare. Heaven directed Anne to illustrate each particular topic by assignment. These are not based on actual people or mystical experiences, but on Anne's personal observations of life.

The Bid

Christopher Murphy turned the key in the ignition of his truck. The engine sprang to life and hummed. The young builder listened appreciatively to the steady sound, comparing it to his last truck, which had always needed coaxing to start. He pulled away from the restaurant in deep thought.

The voice of Terry Black, with whom he had just met, played over and over again in his head. The man made sense in his contention that Christopher would be foolish not to outbid a competitor on a piece of land. He would lose the project if he didn't. Sure, there were other projects, but this one would put Christopher in a higher league and he knew it.

His competition for the piece of land was a former partner, Joe Zimmerman, a man who worked honestly and fairly. Christopher thought back to the breakfast meeting he had just left.

"Get me a little more coffee, honey," Terry Black said to the waitress. "Chris, buddy, I'm trying to help you here. You need to increase your bid. Don't ask me how I know this. One thing you'll learn about me is that I can keep a secret. If you don't adjust your bid, you'll lose this project."

Chris rubbed his eyes in concentration and glanced down at his Timex watch. "Terry, those bids are sealed. The only way you could know this is…"

Terry held up a hand to stop him. "Don't say anything stupid, Chris. You're wet behind the ears in this business and I understand that. I'm your friend."

Chris, feeling naïve, tried to think quickly. If Terry was telling the truth, then someone in the municipal building department was leaking numbers to him. A feeling of nausea began in Christopher's stomach.

The waitress brought two plates of steak and eggs, refusing to make eye contact with either man. Chris wondered if they had somehow offended her.

Terry surveyed the table and spoke impatiently, "I'm still using ketchup on my eggs there, honey, so maybe you could bring some." The young woman turned silently and stalked away. Terry rolled his eyes.

"Just what I need in the morning…a waitress with an attitude. I come here every morning and eat the same thing. You'd think the bimbo would learn to bring ketchup. Okay, Chris, if you want to hang in the big leagues, you better learn how to play ball. I've got a proposition for you."

Chris ate slowly and listened. If there was one thing he knew how to do, it was listen, especially to someone like Terry Black.

"You want to put up two 12-flats, right? You need that site to do it. I'll make sure you get the site and the variance for the parking lot, which will bring you into compliance with the zoning board. See, I have a few friends on the zoning board. I can grease that for you. But you have to outbid Zimmerman by at least ten thousand."

"My bid is in, Terry," Chris responded. "There's nothing I can do."

Terry chuckled. "I saw your bid, buddy. It's just low enough to blow the deal for you. I can pull it and submit the new numbers if you get them to me by noon today."

Chris tried to hide his discomfort. This was disappointing, to say the least. The job, which would be his biggest to date, would make Chris and his wife enough to live on and fund an even bigger project. In two years time, his wife would be finished with nursing school and working part-time. This would get them the health insurance that was costing the Murphys so much.

On the flip side, Joe Zimmerman was no stranger to Chris. He had worked with him for years and knew him to be a good guy. Clearly, Joe's bid for the land had been higher than Chris'.

"Terry, I am grateful to you," Chris began. "Don't think I don't appreciate what you're doing for me. But do you mind if I ask why you are doing this for me?"

Terry gave a loud laugh. "Chris, buddy, you're a straight shooter. I like that in a guy. You know how to call a spade a spade. That's why you're going to do well in this town." He put down his knife and fork and leaned in, lowering his tone of voice.

"Chris, there is more at stake here than you know. I can't tell you everything, but let's just say that things aren't always what they seem. There's going to be a change in zoning on the big parcel of land on the West Side. There's a development company looking to put a mall there. I happen to know that they're looking for a local builder. Now you're young, but I see a lot of potential in you. I think you could handle a project on that level." He stopped, for effect, staring intently at Chris. "You get my drift, Chris. There would be a lot of money for everyone. I mean, let's face it. You don't want to bang nails your whole life, do you?"

Terry Black checked his Rolex watch and spoke quickly. "Your biggest problem would be picking the right suit for the opening dinner."

Chris' head reeled with the possibilities. Something niggled at him. "And why are you doing this for me?"

"Do I have to draw you a picture? If you play ball here, we'll help you out. By we I mean the municipality. Let's say you get this bid and you appreciate my help. You shoot

$45,000 my way as a gesture of appreciation. This is small change. Your profit on these two buildings will be upwards of...what...$700,000? You'd be happy to do that for me, wouldn't you? I'll spread that around a little, you know, to my buddy on the zoning board and maybe even throw Tony a few grand for his re-election fund."

Chris thought quickly. Tony had to be Anthony Valente, the town mayor.

"You help us out, we'll help you. Your old buddy Joe Zimmerman thinks small. We don't see the potential in him like we see it in you."

Trying to act comfortable and relaxed, Christopher kept his voice nonchalant. "I worked with Joe Zimmerman for a few years. He's not a bad guy, Terry."

Terry raised his hands expansively. "We like him, too, Chris. It's just that he doesn't have the big picture. That's all I'm saying." He shook his head innocently. "I've got nothing against him, Chris. We all have families, you know?"

Chris nodded. "Terry, the bids are in. If Joe's is higher, it seems to me that he wins, fair and square."

Terry nodded his head in agreement but Chris detected a narrowing of his eyes. "That would be true, sure as we're both sitting here. I guess what you have to decide, Chris, is if you want to be a builder or a Boy Scout." He chuckled again, to take the sting from his words. "I know this all seems underhanded to you. Maybe you're thinking that this is unfair to Joe."

Chris nodded. It was abundantly clear to him that this was unfair to Joe.

"Look at it this way, Chris," Terry Black reasoned. "You can walk away from this and let Joe have it. But Joe doesn't have what it takes to pull off a project like this. And he damn sure couldn't do the mall job. You, on the other hand, have the moxie to work on this level. You're not small potatoes. You're a smart guy, quick on your feet, and you can handle yourself in high circles. If you walk away from this and let Joe have it, from some naïve idea that you're playing fair, he might blow the whole thing and jeopardize his business. You worked with him. He can't even do math, for God's sake. Chris, you're protecting him from himself."

Chris considered this. There was some truth to this argument. Joe was not exceptionally intelligent. But he worked hard and treated his crews fairly. The men who worked for him developed great loyalty to him. When Joe and Chris worked together, Joe always handled their staff because he had a way with them. But he was not smooth when it came to working with the zoning boards and politicians.

Terry's eyes bored into his own. "Be realistic. You're saving him from a mistake."

Chris nodded, saying nothing. Terry pushed back his plate. "Look at it this way. You like the guy? Then you can take care of him yourself when you get the mall job. And don't think I don't respect that you remember your friends. You're a good man, Chris. We'll take care of you." Terry checked his watch again and rose. "I gotta go, buddy. I'm late for a meeting with Tony. I'll be in my office until noon. You get me that new bid by then and I'll make it happen for you." He glanced out the window. "Is that your blue pickup?"

Chris nodded. The truck was a new-to-him second hand but a huge step up from what he had been driving last month.

Terry smiled down at him. "I've got a friend with a car dealership if you want to trade up. He'll fix you up with a new model for even exchange if I ask him. Let me know if you want me to give him a call." He winked at Chris. "Like I said, we take care of each other."

Terry left the restaurant, leaving Chris with his barely touched steak and eggs. The waitress appeared to clear Terry's plate and Chris put his hand in his pocket for his wallet.

"It's paid for," she snapped.

Back in his truck, Christopher tried to consider his options. There was logic in what Terry said. Chris could take this job and when he landed the mall job he could pull Joe in on it. Joe would never know. And it was possible that Joe wasn't up for the job. There was truth in that.

A little voice told Chris that what he was considering was not only unfair, but underhanded, sneaky, and sly. He mulled it over in his head. One thing was for sure. Joe Zimmerman would never work well with Terry Black. Chris knew Joe Zimmerman and knew that Joe had a low opinion of Terry and Terry's group.

Joe was a bit of a Boy Scout, he thought, when all was said and done. And if this was the way things worked, then who was he to buck the system? He had a family to support, after all. This Terry was a bit of a bully, it was true, but didn't he say that they all had families? He couldn't be that bad if he cared about his family.

Chris weighed it all. He considered talking it over with his wife but decided not to. Collette would not weigh in favorably on Terry Black and Chris knew it. She liked Joe Zimmerman and his wife. No, Chris would have to figure this out by himself.

In his home, his wife Collette prayed as she folded laundry. "Guardian angels," she prayed, "protect my husband."

"I need help," prayed Christopher's guardian angel. Christopher was a good man, but this was a serious temptation. Christopher's angel knew that Christopher was about to step onto a path that could divert him and his family from God's will for many years. This would be bad for the Kingdom.

Saint Michael arrived immediately, with another angel. The two assessed the situation in a second.

"Don't worry," St. Michael assured Christopher's guardian angel. "His wife is praying and his former partner is praying." Glancing at his companion, Michael made a request. "Prompt Christopher's wife to call him."

The angel disappeared and St. Michael and Christopher's angel bowed their heads in prayer. A moment later, the assistant returned looking relaxed.

"Done."

"I have to admit, I was a little surprised to see you show up," Christopher's angel said to St. Michael. "What's going on here?"

St. Michael responded calmly. "It's his son."

"Will he be a priest?" the angel asked.

"No," St. Michael responded. "A politician."

Christopher's angel raised his eyebrows in surprise and Michael smiled. "If Christopher's son is given the right formation, God will use him powerfully."

The guardian angel understood. No wonder Christopher was getting it from all over.

Christopher drove on into the morning, puzzling over this dilemma. His cell phone rang and he answered it in distraction.

"Hi," said his wife, Collette. "What are you doing?"

"Uh, just driving. Thinking about this bid."

"Well, don't worry too much about it. If you don't get this one, you'll get another piece of land. Want to hear my news?"

"Sure. Are we being sued for back taxes?"

Collette laughed. "Not today. I got a letter saying that I received a grant for $8,000. This is based on my school status as a continuing education student with children under the age of five."

Christopher's mouth dropped open. "Are you kidding me?"

Collette laughed in delight. "No. I'm looking at it right now. I applied for it last year. I didn't want to tell you because it was such a long shot. I wasn't going to tell you until tonight but it just occurred to me that wherever you were, you were worrying about money. This will pay for our health insurance until I'm working part-time. Then it will be free. How do you like that?"

"I like that," Christopher admitted. "I like it a lot. How would you like to join the Country Club?"

"What?"

"I had breakfast with Terry Black. He said maybe he would sponsor us to join the Country Club."

"Why would we join the Country Club? Leave me out. That man is slippery." There was a moment's silence. "Stay away from him, Chris. I have a very bad feeling about him. That type of guy wants to own you." More silence. "Patty Zimmerman called. They want us to come to dinner on Friday. I think you should consider working with Joe again. He's so honest, Chris. You two made a good team."

Christopher groaned inside. This was torture. "We'll see. Great news about the grant."

"Yes. This solves our problems."

They hung up and Christopher drove on, irritated. It was good news but it wasn't the Country Club and a contract to build a mall. Collette thought small, like Joe. She would never endorse a bribe.

Christopher brought himself up short. The word had shocked him out of his stupor. He would be bribing Terry Black. Granted, Terry was a lawyer, not technically an official. But he had told Christopher clearly what he intended to do with the money. This was not only immoral, it was illegal. Christopher could go to jail for it.

Terry had said he knew how to keep his mouth shut. Who would know, other than Terry? These things had to be proved. Christopher could write the bid up himself. Collette wouldn't have to know. He considered this for the briefest moment. Collette would know because Joe's wife would tell her what they bid after Christopher secured the land. He would have to get Collette to lie.

Suddenly the clouds parted and Christopher experienced a moment of clarity. He stared at the red light that had stopped him without him seeing it. A lump formed in his throat and he identified an unusual urge to pray. He saw himself, trying to figure out how to trick his wife into lying to her friend. He had identified her with Joe Zimmerman, he knew, not because they both thought small. If Joe Zimmerman thought small, as Terry said, he wouldn't be bidding on a project of this magnitude. Certainly Collette had the highest hopes and expectations for Christopher's business. These two people did not think small, Christopher knew. They thought honestly.

At that moment, Christopher knew he would reject Terry's offer. It would not fit with Collette and it would not fit with Joe Zimmerman.

A rush of calm peace filled Christopher as he realized that it did not fit with him either.

The Three Friends

After finishing her workout, Irene slammed her locker shut and clicked the lock. Samantha and Karen must be running late, she thought, heading for the steam room. Irene worked out with these two women every Wednesday. Friends from college, the three women had little time together anymore because of their respective careers. Wednesdays at the gym enabled them to remain connected.

Irene settled in for a steam, trying to relax her muscles. She had only gotten comfortable when Samantha opened the door, sending a whoosh of steam out.

"Are you here?" Samantha joked, making her way slowly to a bench next to Irene's.

"I'm here," Irene answered. "Is Karen with you?"

Samantha flopped down with a sigh and removed her towel revealing a fashionable bathing suit designed to slenderize. "I'm skipping the workout and going right to the detox," she commented. "No, she's not coming but I just spent an hour talking to her on the phone."

Irene wiped the sweat from her forehead. "Is everything okay with her?"

"No," answered Samantha. "Everything is most definitely not okay with her. She had a disturbing encounter with a positive pregnancy test this morning."

Irene's eyes widened. "Tell me you're joking."

"I wish I was joking," Samantha responded. "She's been feeling weird for awhile. She thought it was stress. I told her that her symptoms sounded kind of consistent with a nine-month condition. She got the test last night and did it this morning."

"That's horrible," Irene whispered. "What is she going to do?"

Samantha shifted, trying to get comfortable on the plastic bench. "What can she do? It's not like she's been with this guy for a long time. He'll want no part of it."

"You don't know that, Samantha," Irene objected. "She has to tell him and see what he says."

"Please. He'll say 'Karen who?' "

"Maybe," admitted Irene. "But she really likes this guy. Maybe it will work out."

Samantha rolled her eyes. "How, Irene? How can this possibly work out? She's twenty-five. She just got this job and is finally working in her field with some hope of advancement. She can hardly start making noises about maternity leave. They'll put her on the Mommy Track. Besides, this guy isn't going to help her."

Irene interrupted, "If he can sleep with her, he can help support the baby."

"Baby? What baby? She's not going to have a baby."

The two women looked at each other in silence. A long moment passed. Irene, a Catholic, had not been to Mass or Confession since high school, with the exception of weddings and funerals.

Samantha made no secret of her feminist leanings.

"Irene," Samantha spoke in a warning voice, "do not inflict your religious beliefs on Karen. This is going to be hard enough for her."

"Pardon me?" Irene replied, offended. "Just because I said the word, baby, I'm a religious fanatic? Karen just took a pregnancy test and it was positive. If nobody else is thinking about a baby, then I must be the only one not in denial."

Samantha spoke in a measured voice. "She can get this taken care of. We know lots of girls who have done this and it's not the end of the world. She can't possibly have a baby right now."

Irene worked hard to remain calm and to keep her voice level. "That's not true, Samantha. She could have a baby now if she wanted. I'm not saying she has to. I'm saying you should not talk to her like it's impossible. Lots of girls we know got pregnant and had their babies and they're doing fine."

Samantha spoke in a patronizing tone. "Irene, just because the Church says that women should remain hostages to their bodies doesn't mean that all women are stupid enough to buy it. Women can think for themselves. They have the right to choose."

Now Irene bristled. "What does this have to do with the Church? I didn't say anything about the Church. All I'm saying is that if Karen is pregnant, she has to make a choice. The word choice implies more than one option. It IS a choice, Samantha, remember?"

"That's right. It is. And it's her choice. So let's try to leave some old man in Rome out of it."

Irene blew hard at the steam and fought back tears. Every time these issues came up she found herself forced to defend a Church she knew little about. This was not about the Church. It was about Karen's baby.

"Samantha," she reasoned, trying another tack. "Wouldn't we like to see what Karen's baby would be like? I mean, maybe it would be a good thing for her. Laura Salyers has a beautiful little boy. He's in Kindergarten now. They're doing fine."

"Yeah, and look how long it took her to finish college. She can't take the job she wants, and she has to work close to home. And this is different. Karen's career is just taking off. And Irene, it's not a baby. Stop calling it that. It's a small blob of tissue that they just scrape out long before it ever becomes a baby. Besides, her family would never support her. Karen's parents would be embarrassed to death to have an illegitimate grandchild."

"They'd get used it," Irene guessed. "People do all the time."

"Irene, I know we've been through this before. You have to understand that abortion is a woman's choice. It's her body. She has the right to decide what to do with it. It's not like she wants this baby. This baby is not wanted. Don't you understand that?"

"Samantha, how many of us were wanted? I don't think every pregnancy leaves every woman delighted. But they get used to it. Our mothers probably didn't plan us. Have you ever thought about that?"

"Our mothers were slaves," Samantha snapped. "And our fathers did whatever they darn well pleased. How was that fair?"

Irene tried to push away at the murky cobwebs that always seemed to descend upon her when she was debating Samantha. Irene sensed that her friend's logic was flawed, but she had a hard time identifying the untruths.

"Our fathers did their best," Irene reasoned. "At least they supported us and stayed. How many fathers today are gone? How many mothers are raising kids by themselves?"

"Exactly," Samantha snapped. "Just like Karen will be if you don't stay out of it."

This stung. "I'm not in it and neither are you," she retorted. "It's up to Karen. And a live kid with a single mother is better than a dead kid if you ask me."

"It's not a kid!" Samantha shouted.

"Yes, it is!" Irene shouted back.

The women glared at each other, aware that they were nearing a line that could not be crossed if they were to maintain their friendship. Both took deep breaths and remained momentarily silent.

"You look like you're losing weight," Irene offered as an olive branch. Samantha fought a continual battle with her weight.

"Yeah, the exercise program seems to be helping. I'm not really losing weight, though. Maybe I'm gaining muscle."

Both laughed at this. Karen used to say this to console them following any unwanted weight gain. In the first year of college Samantha had gained a great deal of weight abruptly. One day she commented on it, verbalizing her distress. Seeking to console her friend, who was fully twenty pounds heavier in three months, Karen had said, "It's all the walking you're doing, Samantha. You're not really gaining weight; you're gaining muscle, which is heavier." This had become a private joke among the friends.

"Don't say anything to her," Samantha advised. "Let her bring it up to you."

"I won't."

"She'll tell you anyway. I think she is in shock right now."

Irene nodded. "Did she go to work?"

"No. She called in sick. She's trying to get an appointment at the clinic on 35th street."

Irene nodded. Karen had made the decision if she was looking for an appointment at a clinic that performed abortions. Feeling deflated and helpless, Irene knew that the moment she escaped Samantha's company she would start to cry. She allowed Samantha to change the subject and Irene wondered if she truly fit in anywhere.

Irene's guardian angel watched with compassion. Irene did not fit in with the circle of friends she had chosen. The angel knew the pain of her isolation but understood that God needed Irene in pain so she would reject the world and choose Him. God had such plans for Irene. The guardian angel watched Irene leave the gym. Offering a prayer for extra grace, he went on ahead of her.

The young mother bundled her two children into snow gear. Just as she finished dressing them, she smelled a dirty diaper and groaned. In the seventh month of her third pregnancy, Susie found it increasingly more and more difficult to get her two and four-year olds into their car seats. Daily Mass meant everything to Susie, though, and she knew that at the end of the pregnancy and for a period right after the birth of this next infant, she would miss Mass. Susie wrestled with the temptation to remain home in the warm house. In the end, the lure of the Eucharist won and she quickly began the process of stripping off the snowsuit to change the diaper.

Cramps shot down her back to her legs as she left the house. Once the children were buckled into their seats, she remembered the packet of pro-life materials she had left by the door. She had promised to put them in the back of the church this morning. Susie groaned again and debated whether or not to get out of the car and go back for them. Offering it up for the poor souls in purgatory, she got out of the car and lumbered back up the six porch stairs to grab the envelope.

"All for You, Lord Jesus," she prayed silently. "Please help some woman who is considering abortion today."

Back in the car, she felt her spirits lift as she drove through the winter morning. Susie always felt she had overcome something once she actually got the kids in the car and left for Mass. The children began to sing in the backseat and Susie joined in.

In the church vestibule the young mother gave her four-year-old the envelope of pro-life materials to hold so the child would not run into the church without her. Susie pulled out the poster of the development of a newborn and showed her children. They admired the pictures of the infant as she thumbtacked the poster onto the bulletin board. Susie's parish priest was active in the pro-life movement and she had promised him she would get the materials into the church. Underneath the poster, Susie placed a stack of pro-life brochures and flyers, offering another prayer that each would be accompanied by heavenly graces.

With a sigh of relief, she pulled her two children into the baby room and sat down heavily to enjoy what she could of the Mass.

Later that afternoon, Irene got into her car and turned the heat on full. She shivered as she headed for home through the early evening darkness. Halfway there, the engine began to sputter. Irene pumped the gas pedal. It sputtered again and died out completely as she pulled over to the side of the road.

"Now what," she muttered to herself. What a horrible day. The image of Karen haunted her and for some reason she kept imagining Karen's baby.

"It's not my problem," she mumbled to herself as she put the car in park and tried to start it. The engine turned over but would not hold the start and she sat back in frustrated helplessness. She pulled her cell phone from her purse and called her father who, mercifully, answered on the first ring.

"I'll be there in thirty minutes," he promised. "Walk over to the restaurant around the corner from there and get something to eat. It's too cold to sit in the car."

Irene agreed and locked her car. She walked to the corner as snow began to blow around her. She felt a sense of foreboding. There were no lights on in the restaurant and the parking lot was nearly empty. Sure enough, the door was locked and a sign in the window informed her that the management was remodeling. Irene pulled gloves from her pocket and put them on. Glancing around, she saw a church across the street. The lights were on and people walked in. Irene hurried in the direction of warmth.

It had been nearly a year since she had been to Mass and Irene blessed herself with holy water and went in to pray. Evening Mass had just begun and she listened to the readings. St. Paul talked about his responsibility to preach the Gospel. Irene closed her eyes and thought again of Karen's baby. It occurred to her that she, like Paul, might have some responsibility to God and to Karen's baby.

Her mind recoiled. It was none of her business what Karen did with her baby. Irene thought of the hurtful comments made by Samantha. Irene pictured the Pope. His face always radiated goodness. Suddenly, she felt ashamed. She should have defended him. She should have talked about his goodness and his humanitarian efforts. She should have said exactly how she felt to Samantha. But what did she feel?

Confused, Irene fought back tears. She thought of religous people as holy rollers and she was not sure about everything the Church taught. Didn't birth control have a place in modern society? Shouldn't women be allowed to choose when and if they wanted to have a baby? These things confused Irene. She figured she was on the fence about them.

One thing that did not confuse her was abortion. No matter what anyone said to the contrary, Irene did not think that it was right to terminate a pregnancy. The very word appalled her. It implied the end of something, the destruction of something. Try as she might, Irene could not reconcile the aggressive contention of her friend that abortion was acceptable.

Irene did not receive Communion, as she knew she needed to go to Confession. She prayed to God silently as others filed past her.

"God, I'm sorry for being so bad. I know you probably don't even listen to someone like me who never prays and never comes to church. I don't blame You. It's just that I don't fit in anywhere. I'm not real religious but I believe in You. Help me, Jesus. And please help Karen. Make her see that she might want to keep her baby. If You want me to talk to Karen, God, I will, but You have to make it really clear to me. You have to show me what to do." Satisfied that she had communicated her feelings, she paused. "I'm sorry I'm not better, God."

Tears again burned her eyes as she rose to leave. The ball was in God's court. If God wanted her to talk to Karen, He would have to give her a sign. Irene walked out into the cold night and looked down the street. Her car sat against the curb, gathering snow on its windshield. Her father was nowhere in sight. A gust of bitterly cold wind forced her back into the vestibule of the church. She saw the bulletin board and went over to have a look.

The first thing she saw was the poster of an infant developing in the womb.

Irene's mouth dropped open and grace washed over her soul. She felt the presence of Christ clearly and profoundly. The brochure resting below the poster gave pictures of each stage of development and suddenly Irene knew how she would talk to Karen. Now she did not fight the tears. She looked at the picture of the eight-week old preborn baby and allowed the tears to stream down her face. Irene cried for Karen, yes, but she also cried in joy because God had heard her prayer and answered it immediately.

In that moment, Irene knew that Jesus loved her and

accepted her as she was. Perhaps she did not know exactly where she fit in on earth but Irene knew with a glowing certainty that she fit in with Jesus Christ.

Maybe I don't need to fit in here in the world, she thought. Maybe I need to stand out.

Irene saw the line of people waiting for Confession. Stuffing the brochure into her purse, she went back into the church and took her place in line. It was time to get off the fence.

The Brown Jacket

Marcella hastily poured herself a glass of wine. It had been a horrid day. The landscape designer cancelled again. Shannon's graduation party was two weeks from Saturday and unless there was a miracle, the garden would not be finished.

Additionally, Marcella's haircut was wrong. The new stylist highly recommended by a friend had been a disaster. Marcella glanced at the mirror alongside the telephone on the wall and wrinkled her nose in distaste. The top was poufy.

Examining the wallpaper, she allowed herself to be comforted. The color of the border worked perfectly with the new paint. The kitchen designer had more than earned her money. The inside of the house was coming along just fine, Marcella thought, running her hand over the granite countertop. She sighed and pulled out meat for dinner. George, her husband, would be home momentarily.

Marcella ran the steaks under water and switched on the oven to bake potatoes. Thoughts of her husband prompted her to pour another glass of wine. Marcella could hardly remember a time when she actually liked George. Sure, he worked hard. So did a lot of people. George cared about George, she felt. He did what he wanted.

George would argue that he provided for the family and was entitled to relaxation time. George liked to play golf. A lot. He had a circle of friends who also played golf and they travelled to tournaments. Marcella knew that they drank heavily on these outings. She also suspected they did other things. A long time ago she stopped caring.

Shannon and Danny, their children, were what counted,

Marcella knew. It was important that the children have a stable family, even if there was little love lost between the parents. Marriages were not all perfect, Marcella told herself. A woman learned to console herself in other ways. Marcella flipped through the pages of a magazine and spotted a line of clothing that might suit her. She picked up the phone and called her girlfriend, sharing the story of the tragic haircut and asking her what she knew about this clothing line. They agreed to have lunch the next day, following a brief shopping excursion to the mall that featured the clothing.

Marcella hung up and sighed heavily. She opened up the box from the bakery to set out the dessert. There were 12 doughnuts instead of the apple tarts she had ordered. Frustration filled her. Hadn't she specifically told the girl to be certain it was her order in the box? This was the second time this had happened. She could hardly drive back to the bakery. The young girl had not listened to her. Marcella slammed the cover of the box shut and picked up the phone, dialing the bakery.

The phone was answered on the second ring and Marcella jumped right in to the manager.

"This is Mrs. Ryan," she began. "I ordered six apple turnovers. I specifically asked that the girl check the box to be certain this was my order. This has happened before and I am not tolerating it. I will stop using your bakery and I will tell my friends to stop using your bakery. That girl is incompetent."

The manager apologized and offered to replace the items for free the following day. Marcella hung up and felt a little better. They would not push her around.

George came in the door and grunted in response to her greeting. Marcella opened her magazine again as he made himself a drink. George took his drink into the living room and turned on the news. Marcella sighed again as she put the steaks in the broiler. She struggled with the broiling pan and finally gave it a violent push to engage it. She should buy a new oven, she thought. The color did not work with the new kitchen anyway. Marcella had seen the latest models a few days ago. She resolved right then to get one. She would pick it out tomorrow afternoon.

The front door slammed and Danny and Shannon arrived home.

"Put your backpacks under the stairs," Marcella ordered. She hated picking up their things. It seemed she no sooner got the house in order than they arrived home, scattering possessions everywhere. The housekeeper was next to useless. She just piled things in corners. Marcella exhausted herself trying to get her money's worth from that woman.

"How was school?" she asked in a flat voice.

"Fine," answered thirteen-year-old Shannon. "Ask Danny."

"Danny, how was school?" Marcella asked.

"Fine," he answered shortly, heading up the stairs to his room.

"He hit a kid," Shannon informed her mother. "He has detention on Saturday."

"Did you hear that, George?" Marcella called into the living room. "Danny got in a fight at school."

"Don't make it a drama, Marcella," her husband answered in a bored voice. "Boys will be boys."

Marcella suppressed a wave of anger. "What happened, Shannon?"

Shannon opened the fridge and stared inside. Marcella submerged more anger. Why did her children stare into the fridge, letting all the cold air out? And they never put anything back where it belonged. Marcella constantly had to reorganize the contents of the refrigerator.

"All I know is that he got in big trouble," Shannon

reported. "He pushed a kid against the wall and the kid's head banged off the bricks. The kid was bleeding."

Marcella took a gulp of her wine and tried to think of something to say.

"That's terrible. Was he in the principal's office? Do you think they'll be calling here?"

Shannon finally selected a can of pop and slammed the door, shaking the whole appliance.

"Duh. I kind of think so," she answered. "The kid was crying and they had ice on his head. Danny was really pissed off."

"Watch your language, Shannon," Marcella snapped in annoyance. Why did they think it was okay to speak this way?

Shannon rolled her eyes.

"Why did Danny hit him?"

Shannon shrugged her shoulders. "I don't know. Maybe because he's a psycho."

George entered the kitchen and got himself another drink.

"George, the child was bleeding," Marcella informed him. "They had to ice his head. This is not the first time Danny has been in a fight."

"He's not in fights, Mom," Shannon piped in. "He's beating people up."

"Everything's a drama," George said in disinterest. "Kids fight, Marcella. Don't make it an international incident."

He left the room. Marcella gritted her teeth and turned to take out the dishes to set the table.

"Can I stay over at Sandy's on Friday night?" Shannon asked.

Marcella breathed in hard. "I don't know," she answered. "I don't think it's a good idea. Her parents are never home."

"Mom," Shannon whined. "Who cares? You guys are never home and they let her stay here."

Marcella whirled around and slammed her hand on the table. "Don't you dare talk to me like that, Shannon. Get up to your room and do your homework."

Shannon stalked from the room in anger.

At that moment the phone rang. Marcella deliberately ignored it and after the fifth ring, her husband picked it up. She heard his end of the conversation and breathed a sigh of relief that she had not taken the call. It was Danny's teacher, relating the incident of the fight. After a few minutes, the conversation ended and Marcella waited. George said nothing.

Finally Marcella went into the living room.

"Who was that?"

"Danny's teacher," he answered.

"What did she say?"

"She told me about the fight."

"What did you tell her?"

"I told her I'd talk to him."

"Well, are you going to talk to him?"

George slammed his glass down in irritation. "Do you have to nag me? Can I sit down for ten minutes when I get home? It's not the end of the world. He's got a bad attitude because you give him whatever he wants. That's the problem, Marcella."

"I do not," she retorted. "And how would you know? You're never here."

"Here we go again," he intoned. "Poor Marcella. Her bad husband leaves her alone and she can't cope with two kids."

"I just think it might be helpful if you actually spent some time with him, George. Is that too much to ask?"

Raising his voice, her husband slammed down the glass he had just picked up. "He's got everything. What the hell does he want? He has more than I ever had. Maybe if he had to work a little he would appreciate what he has."

"George, he's ten. Do you want him to get a job?"

"It might not be a bad idea."

Marcella shook her head in frustration and retreated to the kitchen. George made no sense. She could never get any help from him. If she forced him to take responsibility for disciplining the kids, he would do it wrong just to discourage her from asking. She checked the steaks and defiantly poured herself another glass of wine.

The phone rang again. This time Shannon picked up the extension upstairs. Shortly after, she ran down.

"Mom," she said in a hurry. "It's Sandy. Her older sister is buying tickets for the Omnimax theater on Saturday night. I'd have to stay over. Can I go? Please?"

Marcella pulled the steaks out of the oven and answered in a flat voice. "Sure. Go ahead."

Marcella awakened early the next morning, as she had for the last two weeks. She knew from experience that she would be unable to get back to sleep. The heaviness that weighed on her was not just the result of the extra glass of wine but she went down to the kitchen and reached for aspirins anyway. It all helped.

Danny was troubled, she knew. Shannon had withdrawn from her parents. George was in his own little world and she had given up trying to reach him. Sometimes it was easier to play the game without making waves. Depression threatened to immobilize Marcella and she filled the coffee pot, staring at the red "On" light. Maybe if she stood there, motionless, she would get some inspiration. She was running away from her children and she knew it. When had it happened? At some point in the last two years, Marcella had switched off.

She poured herself the first cup of coffee and sat down heavily at the table.

It could be worse, she thought. They could all be down here looking at me for something.

That was the problem, she thought. Marcella felt empty, as though she had nothing to give. Laying her head down on the table, she began to cry.

"Help me," she prayed silently. "Somebody help me."

Marcella's guardian angel sprang into prayer. "St. Therese," he prayed. "She's ready for help."

St. Therese, the Little Flower, appeared at once and smiled at the angel. "Well done. Where is the novena card?"

The angel understood immediately. "It's in the jacket of the coat she wore to Danny's First Holy Communion. The front hall closet."

Therese looked compassionately at Marcella. "Put it in her hands today and I'll do the rest."

The angel joyfully agreed. "I've been waiting for this day."

Therese smiled again. "So has God. We won't disappoint Him. Let's pray that God grant her clarity and the courage to change."

Marcella pulled herself together. Something had to change. Something would change, she vowed. From somewhere, she felt the smallest stirring of courage and she lifted her head up because of it.

Marcella could not control George. She had tried for years to pull him into his role in the family. Fine. She had to accept that she could not change him and work on herself instead. She thought back to the evening before and what she had said to the manager of the bakery. Her face flushed. How appallingly she had behaved. She shook her head hard. The word "change" kept coming into her head. She would stop running from her children. Danny needed George. They all did. But if George refused to spend time with them, Marcella would have to do the best she could by herself. It was time for change.

Getting the children out the door in the morning presented Marcella with her biggest challenge every day. They could never find their things.

"Let's go, Danny," Shannon shouted. "You always make me late."

Danny sat at the table, writing furiously.

Marcella looked at his bowed head and noted that he badly needed a haircut. "What are you doing, Danny?"

"My homework. What does it look like?"

Marcella ignored the jibe and reproached herself. This should have been done last night but after the third glass of wine Marcella had not cared about homework.

"Are you almost done?"

"Yeah."

"Shannon, get in the car and buckle up. We'll be out in a minute."

Shannon banged open the screen door and stomped out in anger. Change, thought Marcella. We're all going to change. She waited patiently while Danny finished his homework and then helped him to pack his backpack.

"I have a half-day today," he reminded her. "Can you pick me up?"

Looking down at his little face, she felt such remorse. How many days had she allowed the babysitter to pick him up because she was busy?

"You bet," she answered, thinking of her shopping and lunch date. "I'll be there. We're going to go and get you a haircut. How about that?"

He smiled and her heart lifted. "Great," he answered.

"What else are we going to do?"

She picked up his backpack and headed him toward the closet for his jacket. "It'll be a surprise to both of us because we don't have any plans. We'll just see what happens."

Danny laughed at this and Marcella's spirits lifted even more.

The light in the closet had burned out and Marcella could not find the brown jacket she wore each day. She rummaged through all the coats a second time. It wasn't there. A loud insistent honking came from the driveway and she felt a wave of anger at Shannon. Did all kids honk at their mothers?

"Mom, wear this one," Danny suggested, pulling a black dress coat from the back.

"It's a dress coat," she protested. Where had her jacket gone? The horn honked again and Danny covered his ears. "Okay. Give it to me, Dan. I'm only going to school and back."

Once the children were dropped off, Marcella headed back home. She felt a quivering hope inside and needed time to examine it. She parked the car in front of the house and stepped into the frosty air. Pushing her hands down into her pockets, she pulled everything out. There was the key to the storage shed that had been missing, along with some Kleenex, a piece of gum, and a holy card. Marcella looked down at the image of St. Therese of Lisieux and felt tears sting her eyes. Her mother had given this card to her at Danny's First Communion. Shortly after, Marcella's mother had died. Tears began to roll down her face and Marcella hurried into the house.

The card featured a novena on the backside. Marcella made another cup of coffee and sat down, staring at this little reminder of her mother.

"Mom," she prayed tearfully. "Please help me. It's a mess down here."

In her heart, Marcella felt the answer and began to say the first day of the novena prayer. As she prayed, she felt courage and determination. When had she stopped praying? Sitting with her coffee, Marcella made decision after decision.

The first call she made was to cancel her lunch date. After that, she resolved to stop drinking in the evenings. Shannon was definitely not staying overnight on Saturday night. Marcella knew that this friend was a bad influence on her daughter. She resolved to be fearless in the face of Shannon's rage.

I know, she thought. I'll take them myself and bring Danny. This was the answer and she smiled to herself.

For some inexplicable reason, Marcella could see her life, her children, and her husband with a clarity that had eluded her for the last two years. Her children needed her. Marcella decided that she would offer the novena up for George. He was the only thing she could not fix so she would turn him over to God. When she made this decision, a lovely calm peace descended upon her soul. She knew God loved her and she knew she was not alone. God would fix this family.

Marcella rose and began to clean her house. After that, she would get in the car and drive to church and officially put the whole mess in the hands of Jesus. The tears continued but these were happy tears, tears of relief.

As she hung up her coat, she felt something under her foot. She bent down and picked up her brown jacket from the floor where it had fallen. How on earth had she missed it?

The Fundraiser

John rummaged in his dresser drawer for the diamond cufflinks. No point setting her off by wearing the wrong ones. He located them and put them on, examining his tuxedo in the mirror. Tonight was important to Christine.

He walked through the dressing room to his wife's bathroom. She sat at her mirror, artfully applying makeup.

"Did you check your shoes?" she asked without looking away from the mirror.

"I did. They're polished. We'll want to leave by seven if we're going to get there a little early."

"I have a clock in front of me, John," she responded. "I know what time we have to leave."

He said nothing but digested her words and tone. Standing behind her, he admired her as he had countless times. John had been struck by Christine's beauty from the moment he first laid eyes on her.

"What are you looking at?"

He smiled. "I'm admiring you in that dress."

"It's nice," she agreed. "You can't go wrong with Dior."

Christine was beautiful, but it was not an effortless beauty, John thought to himself. After their wedding, four years before, he learned that Christine spared no expense or time to look the way she did. It was nearly a full-time job, he considered. There were countless appointments and consultants, all contributing to the finished product in front of him. As had been happening of late, John compared her to a woman he had dated in college. That woman had been every bit as beautiful with no appointments and simple clothing. And she had been pleasant.

John dismissed the thought as unfair. Christine did a lot of important charity work and there was plenty of pressure in it. Feeling guilty, he put his hands on his wife's bare shoulders, giving her an affectionate squeeze.

She froze and stared at him in the mirror. Blue eyes bored into his. "Do you want your hands to be brown?" she asked. "If not, I suggest you take them off me. I have a bronzer on my shoulders."

Feeling foolish, John removed his hands.

"Go wash them," she ordered. "It'll be everywhere if you don't."

He did. To move them past the awkwardness and coldness, John made conversation.

"Did the flowers get sorted?"

"Yes," she answered. "No thanks to anyone on the committee. I had to make three phone calls to get to the bottom of it, but I did. As of this afternoon the tables were ready."

"Good," he answered. "That's good."

"Who is coming from your firm?"

"I'm not sure. They bought two tables. I'm sure a couple of the partners will be there."

Silence greeted this. John worked for one of the most prestigious law firms in the city. Christine often used the affiliation to further her goals. It could be embarrassing but John understood that her philanthropic work required social networking.

"I want to put the mayor with Tom Nelson," she mused. "I worked the seating out accordingly. We'll see what happens. Make sure you introduce the Nelsons to the Hanleys, John."

She looked at him in the mirror again and he agreed. He knew his job. John sat down on the side of the tub, where he could see her.

"Christine, how many more of these projects are you

going to get involved in?"

"Why?"

He chose his words carefully, conscious of the minefield in front of him. "It takes up so much time."

"You object to this?"

"No. I don't object to this, but it's all we do. I just figure that we'll want to do other things in addition to social engagements. If you take on these commitments, it limits us."

"My work is important, John," she retorted coldly. "We can't all spend summers lounging at summer homes."

This was a slap at his family and he felt the water level rising. Before their marriage, John spent a lot of time in the summer at his family's summer estate with his brothers and sisters and their families. Since their wedding, Christine refused to go with him, preferring to remain in the city. She became very displeased if John went alone.

"I respect your work," he assured her. "I'm very proud of what you do. But when we have children, we won't be able to do as much socially. That's all I'm saying."

She remained silent and began to work on her hair, which had been done that afternoon.

"You know?" he pressed.

"We don't have children now, John, so this conversation is irrelevant."

He considered retreating, given her mood, but steeled himself to persevere. When the subject of children arose, Christine was like the artful dodger. John wanted an answer.

"Christine, you're thirty-four and I'm thirty-six. When do you think we'll have children?"

She lay down her brush carefully and turned to face him. "John, why are you doing this to me?"

The water rose by the second. "Doing what?"

"Putting this kind of pressure on me. Do you know how hard I've worked for this night? Do you understand how stressful it is to organize this kind of a function? How dare you challenge me with this right now."

John controlled his temper. "Christine, I think it's a fair question. I'm not trying to put pressure on you. I'm just asking. We're not getting any younger. We're out four nights a week and I'm tired of it. By the time we try to have kids we'll be too old."

Her voice changed and he sensed a shift. "We're not going to be too old, John," she soothed. "There's plenty of time."

John considered. An instinct told him that she was avoiding a fight before the evening's event because she needed him to be charming and affectionate in front of people. He looked at his wife and felt suddenly cold. The coldness originated from her, he suspected. She was like an ice queen. She had not answered his question, but then, she never did. Christine did not have to give him a lot, he mused, just enough to keep him putting on his cufflinks and polished shoes.

John continued to stare at her, his mind darting around. Did this woman in the mirror care about him at all?

"John," she snapped. "John."

"What?" he asked dully, turning his attention to her face.

"Why are you looking like that?"

"Like what?"

"Like you are thinking about something terrible."

"No reason, Christine," he answered, rising. "It just occurs to me that you don't intend to have kids at all."

She threw her brush against the make up table and stood up.

"I knew it," she raged. "I knew you would ruin this night for me. Did you wake up wondering how you were going to destroy this event for me? Or did you just come up with the plan now? Why do you always attack me? Why? You're the most selfish person in the world, John. All you care about is yourself. It's all you, you, you."

John, feeling sick and deflated, began to defend himself. "I'm just asking a question, Christine."

"Asking a question? You're constantly demanding that I get pregnant. Do you think I want to gain fifty pounds? Do you know how hard it is for me to look like this?" She indicated her dress and trim figure. "I'm not going to turn into one of those fat housewives always talking about their spoiled kids. You should have married a brainless twit if you wanted a houseful of brats."

It was like Pandora's box. He knew there'd be no stuffing this tirade back in the bag.

"I work hard for you, John. Do you think you would have gotten promoted if it weren't for my influence?" She gave a derisive laugh. "It wasn't your brains and performance that clinched that promotion. Trust me on that. Half of the partners would have picked someone else. I know that for a fact."

Feeling kicked in the stomach, John turned and walked back through the dressing room to their bedroom, taking off the cufflinks as he went. It was too much. He could not pretend tonight.

Christine came right after him. Seeing him throw his cufflinks onto his dresser, she changed tactics. "John, let's not do this."

"I'm not doing anything, Christine," he answered calmly. "And I'm not going to your fundraiser."

"John," she shrieked, "You started this, not me. You have to go. How will it look if you don't show up?"

He stood, facing the window. He heard the fabric in her dress swish and she moved behind him, putting both her hands on his shoulders.

"You're tired. I forgive you. Let's not fight, John. I know you want a baby and I want one, too. Just not right now. I'm sorry about what I said about your promotion. You just made me so angry attacking me right before this party. I promise we'll talk about the baby tomorrow night at dinner. Okay? I promise."

John's guardian angel exchanged a look with Christine's guardian angel.

Neither was surprised when Mary, the Blessed Mother, appeared next to them. John's mother prayed to Our Lady without cease for her son's marriage. The angels bowed before her even as she greeted them with a sad smile.

"Our poor John is suffering tonight."

They nodded, saying nothing.

"It's time for John to walk down another path," she said gently. "I think now he understands the futility of Christine's way. We'll pray that Christine is willing to follow her husband. I think John could benefit from conversation with some true followers." The angels listened eagerly. How they loved working with Mary. "Can you arrange that for this evening?"

They nodded happily. Christine's guardian angel in particular felt relieved with the extraordinary help. Christine had blocked out heaven for years. Suddenly there was hope.

The fundraiser swelled with attendees as the evening wore on. Christine wore her public face, all smiles, and bubbling with conversation. In his whole life John could not remember feeling this lonely. He stood beside her in the receiving line, also smiling, joining in the conversation when he had to. He noticed Christine's occasional looks of concern. He knew she worried lest he commit the unpardonable sin and quit in the middle of the game.

It has to change, John thought. He could not live like this anymore. Watching Christine, he observed her ability to charm people. She had charisma. John felt a weighty depression settling in on him as he excused himself and walked outside. Standing on the balcony, he looked out at the lights of the city. There had to be more to life than these endless parties.

A hand on his shoulder startled him.

"John? Are you Christine's husband?" asked an elegant woman around his age. "I'm Laura Brandt. This is my husband Evan."

John shook their hands, racking his brains for some recollection of their identity. Sensing his dilemma, Laura Brandt laughed.

"John, there is no way you could remember us," she began. "We were at your wedding. I'm a friend of Christine's from college."

"Of course," John said in relief. "How are you? It's difficult to remember all the faces and names."

"There were over five hundred people at your wedding, John," Evan said in understanding. "You didn't have a hope of remembering them all."

"We just moved back to town," Laura explained. "I heard about the fundraiser and thought it would be the perfect opportunity to get in touch with some old friends."

The couple chatted happily with John and he felt his sense of loneliness ease somewhat. They were warm and genuine and the conversation was easy and true, instead of forced. Christine came through the doors, searching for her husband.

"There you are," she began. He noted again how gracefully

she moved and John knew he loved his wife.

"Laura, you made it," Christine exulted. "And Evan, how are you?"

They exchanged greetings as Christine put her hand on her husband's shoulder. The conversation flowed between the two couples and John felt his spirits lift in spite of himself. Evan had been hired by the mayor to head a task force on police corruption. It was an extremely prestigious appointment and Christine was interested at once. Laura had just had the couple's second baby and was taking time at home.

"We're boring compared to the way we used to live," she stated. "But what can you do? Once the kids come you can't be out all the time."

"We were just talking about that this evening," Christine said, surprising John. "Being out all the time gets old, Laura. You're certainly not missing anything."

The couples talked as long as Christine managed to remain away from her duties and then arranged to meet for dinner the following week. Christine chatted animatedly on the way home, explaining to John that Laura and she had been close in college but then drifted apart.

"She was my closest friend, John," Christine explained. "She got into religion in college but she never made you feel like a sinner. I'm glad they're back."

Maybe there is hope, John thought to himself. These people were nothing like most of Christine's friends. He felt his attention drawn to the key chain hanging from the ignition. On it was the image of Mary, Our Lady of Grace. Heaven seemed to fill the car and John felt flooded with comfort.

His life would change, he knew. He prayed that Christine would change with him.

The Wedding

Vicky watched as the red line darkened on the little stick she held in her hand.

"Oh no," she muttered. "Surely it's wrong."

The pregnancy test showed positive. Vicky was pregnant. She gave a deep sigh and sagged against the door of the bathroom. Patrick was on the other side of the door. There was no telling how he would take this.

She went out and met his concerned eyes.

"It's positive," she said.

Any hope of a good reaction dissipated as Patrick swore under his breath.

"This is a disaster," he stated.

In their late twenties, Patrick and Vicky had been preparing for their wedding for over a year. The date was a tantalizing seven months away.

"Is there any chance…?" he asked.

Vicky shook her head, reading his mind. "I'll be eight months pregnant, Pat. No way. We'll have to…I don't know. Cancel it?"

"Vicky, we can't," he argued. "Do you know how much money we'd lose? My parents would have a fit."

She gazed at him directly. "What should we do?"

He shifted uncomfortably in his seat at the kitchen table. "You could get an abortion."

Vicky felt the air go out of her and she sat down heavily on one of the chairs. This was not going well.

"Vicky," he said persuasively, "this was not in the plan. It will ruin the wedding. Let's have a baby when we're both ready. Besides, the honeymoon is paid for. And what would we tell people?" He shook his head and repeated, "This was not in the plan."

Vicky pushed her brown hair back from her face, leaning her head down to rest on her two hands. No wonder she had been so tired.

"Couldn't we just say we got a head start?"

Patrick snorted. "Get real. Vicky, this is just not what we planned."

Losing her temper, Vicky shouted. "Will you stop talking about what we planned? I KNOW this is not what we planned. But maybe life doesn't always have to be planned."

Patrick's face changed. He spoke gently. "Vicky, we can have a baby later. It's not like we're never going to have kids. But we're not ready now. And the invitations are done. Everything's paid for. This is your dream wedding, for heaven's sake. Vicky, think of your dress, the bridesmaids. Do you want to throw all that away?"

Vicky started to cry. "No. But what about this baby? Can we throw this baby away?"

"It's not a baby," he said coldly. "You don't believe that, do you? I know a lot of women who have had abortions. You're only two months pregnant, for God's sake. It's a blob of tissue."

"Patrick, do you wonder if it's a boy or girl? I mean, do you even wonder?"

He set his mouth stubbornly. "No. I don't. We'll have children later. Vicky, our parents would be furious. They'd be mortified. It would ruin everything. We cannot have a baby now and that's final."

Three weeks later, Vicky lay on her couch, listlessly staring at a soundless television. The abortion had been nearly painless, as promised. All of the arguments had worn her down. It was easier to have the abortion than to argue with Patrick, who had enlisted the aid of her mother. Everything they said made sense. More than anyone, Vicky understood that the pregnancy was inconvenient. She felt a wave of hatred for them both.

"Stop," she scolded herself.

They had both been so kind, really. Patrick had never been so supportive and her mother reminded her that she was lucky to have such a patient fiancé. Her mother explained that having a baby so soon would destroy their first years together. Blah, blah, blah.

She took the remote control and turned up the volume, searching for a distraction. The phone rang. She ignored it. It rang and rang. Vicky pressed the up arrow on the television volume control and held it down as the sound rose higher and higher. When it drowned out the ringing phone she released the button. Wedding talk, once so joyful, nauseated her.

A huge unopened florist package sat on the floor by the door. More roses from Patrick, she suspected. She had not even opened the card. Once, the thought of roses from Patrick had filled her with delight. Now she saw the action as manipulative. He did not care about her or he would have welcomed the baby…whoops…the blob of tissue.

Vicky turned her face away from the pain of her thoughts and went into the kitchen, pulling the now silent phone off the hook as she walked by. She found a prescription bottle of pain killers and took two. Remembering she had not eaten, she opened the door of the refrigerator. A milk carton featured the face of a missing child.

"God help that mother," she prayed, feeling a heart-piercing wave of anguish.

She studied the picture of the child's face. "My child is not missing," she reminded herself aloud. "My child is dead."

Feeling her legs go weak, Vicky sank down onto the floor in front of the refrigerator and sobbed.

In a nearby church, the daily Rosary began, as it always did at this time. An elderly woman with grey hair asked heaven for an end to abortion, as well as healing graces for all those who were suffering from an abortion.

Vicky's guardian angel sat close by, eyes raised, appealing for help. The face of Vicky's angel was solemn in the presence of her despair and the angel appealed to Our Lady, who came immediately.

The Blessed Mother stood close by Vicky. Her calm beauty reassured the angel and filled him with peace.

"Shh, little lamb," Mary whispered to Vicky, bending over her pitiful little form. The Queen of Heaven began to stroke Vicky's head soothingly. "Your child is safe with me in heaven. Shhh. I will keep your daughter for you until you come to us. Hush now, little Vicky. God loves you and God loves your daughter. Tell God you are sorry, Vicky, and He will forgive you."

Mary turned to the angel. Her sorrowful face reflected Vicky's terrible pain. "She will repent," Our Lady said gently. "But there is little to console a mother who has lost a child, particularly in these circumstances. Her grief is deep, but in her brokenness she will find Jesus and learn His compassion. Poor little lamb. God's poor little creatures."

Vicky's sobs began to quiet and she pulled her knees up to her chest and wrapped her arms around them. In a little ball of wounded humanity, Vicky sat in front of the refrigerator and considered. She should have held firm and defended her right to have her baby. Patrick was ready for sex, she thought bitterly, but not for a baby. They should have waited. And her mother? Vicky shook her head in disgust. Her mother cared only about what people thought and Vicky hated her for it. How could her mother not want her baby?

She shook her head against the depth of the betrayal she felt. Vicky considered, for the millionth time, canceling the wedding. The wedding had cost them their first child. How could she ever be happy with Patrick? Her mother talked about their first years together but Vicky could barely stand to look at her future husband. His chattering on about the wedding repulsed her.

She knew she was annoying to him. He looked at her and saw the reproach in her eyes. Vicky did not know how to change that. She could try to act as if nothing happened but what would be the point? Tears came when she opened the refrigerator, for heaven's sake. Vicky could not control her grief.

First her baby had been an unacceptable burden to them and now Vicky found that her grief was unacceptable.

"I hate them," she said aloud.

This made her feel a little better. At least if she said it out loud she could hear it. It made it real and her anger at Patrick and her mother was real, even if they did not find it acceptable. They had not given her a choice.

"I should have been stronger," she told herself again and again.

Vicky considered that if she insisted on having the baby, Patrick would not have left her. He would have eventually coped, despite the disappointment of a ruined wedding. Her mother would have been embarrassed and furious, but so what? Eventually, she too would have had to get over it or risk not seeing her grandchild.

Vicky squeezed her eyes shut at this. A grandchild. She

pictured a small child in a sailor suit. Her mind immediately flashed back to the clinic and she hid her face in her knees.

"I'm sorry," she thought in despair. "Please, God, help me."

The tears came again. Her guardian angel knelt in rapt adoration as the room filled with brightness. Jesus Christ stood beside Vicky. Pure white light radiated from Him as He bent down to encircle her in His arms. The angel, recognizing a moment of profound grace, prayed silently. Love and mercy flowed out from the Savior, filling the room so powerfully that Vicky's sobs quieted and turned to steady crying.

"I'm here, little Vicky," the Savior whispered to her soul. Compassion and love and healing graces flowed from Jesus into Vicky's soul. "You are forgiven, Vicky. I forgive you and I love you. I will take care of you, My little child."

Vicky took her head out from her arms and laid her face on her knees.

"I'm so sorry," she whispered aloud.

"You must begin to forgive yourself, Vicky," Jesus whispered back. "All of heaven will welcome you. You have great things to offer the world. Many souls will be helped by your kindness in the future. But you must forgive yourself or you will never heal. I love you. I need your help. Will you help your Jesus?"

Vicky gave a deep healing sigh. She thought suddenly of other women she knew who were suffering and the most compelling compassion coursed through her. How she loved them all in this moment of agony. Vicky decided, then and there on the kitchen floor, that she would be much kinder to people, especially those who were hurting. If she was in this much pain and nobody knew, how much pain were others suffering? A feeling of determination and strength flooded her soul and she decided something else. She would go to Confession immediately. She would get this off her chest and be done with it. There was no bringing her child back but she could live differently.

She thought of her mother and Patrick and realized that they had also acted in weakness.

Another huge sigh escaped her. She would have to forgive them but it would take time. Vicky felt better. The grief was still there. She still felt pain. But something had changed and she knew she would not die from it. God loved her. She knew this as much as she had ever known anything in her life. God forgave her. She knew this, too.

Vicky made one final resolution before she pulled herself up from the floor. She would call the abortion a mistake. Only by stating the truth, that she had made a mistake, could she come to terms with it. Vicky rose from the floor and calmly put the phone back on the hook.

The Conversation

"I must tell you what I heard last night, Bridget," Karla said as she filled her visitor's cup of tea. "Do you know the new child in my Thomas' class? His mother is from the North Side. Single."

Bridget raised her eyebrows as she added sugar and milk to her cup. "Is she divorced?"

Karla shrugged. "Separated anyway. There's no man in the house. At least not in the permanent sense of the word, if you know what I mean."

Bridget nodded. She understood the implication. "I see her in the mornings at school."

"She dresses kind of fast, don't you think?"

Bridget considered. "I wouldn't wear short skirts to take the kids to school."

Karla shook her head in agreement. "I wouldn't dress that way on a Saturday night, not to mind taking a child to school in the morning. Have you seen her makeup? She must put it on with a paintbrush."

The women laughed.

"It sends a message, Bridget. Don't you think?"

"It can send the wrong message," Bridget agreed.

"I'm just not like that," Karla said virtuously. "I like to look good but I don't spend all my time doing it. Someone who wears short skirts like that is looking for attention. How old do you think she is?"

"I'd say thirty-five," Bridget speculated.

"And dressing like twenty-five and probably behaving like sixteen. Have you seen her son? I don't think she knows where the iron is kept. I could not do that to my children,"

Karla expounded. "What kind of woman sends her child off to school looking so sloppy?"

"One who just doesn't care, I guess," Bridget answered.

"I heard she was making eyes at Marie Campion's husband when she dropped their son off. Marie said she was dressed in high boots and flirting with him."

Bridget reached for the teapot, feeling a little guilty about the conversation but enjoying it at the same time. Karla was not known for discretion.

"What did Marie say she did?"

Karla shrugged impatiently, hesitant to let the truth spoil the story. "It wasn't what she said, but the way she said it." The women exchanged knowing glances. "I would not have her in my house."

"Any word on what happened to the father?"

"Who knows?" Karla answered. "Women today don't care about making a marriage work. They're too selfish. All they care about is clothes and makeup and running around. My Thomas was there last week after school. He said there was beer in the refrigerator and not much else. Apparently she fed them a frozen pizza." Karla rose to check her soup on the stove. "I am very careful to give my children a balanced diet. I'm not afraid of the kitchen like some people."

Bridget agreed. "You are a good cook, Karla. You know how to run a house."

Karla accepted the compliment with lowered eyes, pretending humility. "It's just that so many children are overweight because their mothers do not cook. I could never do that to my children."

Bridget sipped her tea. "It's sad, really."

Karla agreed. "You're a good cook, Bridget."

Bridget, face a mask of seriousness, responded firmly. "Children need to eat right. I don't allow eating between meals or any junk food in my house. It spoils their appetites."

"Do you see what they bring in their lunches, some of these kids?"

"It's a disgrace," Bridget agreed.

"Bad mothers." Karla pronounced. The two lapsed into a temporary silence.

"Did you hear about Agnes Worthington's mother?"

Bridget shook her head. "No."

Karla tried to hide her delight at being the one to share this piece of news. "She's pregnant again."

Bridget's eyes widened. "That had to be a surprise."

"More like a shock," Karla agreed. "The woman never wanted the two she has, not to mind another one."

"How far along is she?"

"She's showing so I'd guess four or five months."

"Is she still working?"

Karla nodded furiously. "Of course. That baby will be lucky if she takes a day off to deliver. Those kids are raising themselves over there."

"Her job is hard," Bridget agreed, feeling a little defensive of the woman as she herself also worked. "Her husband works from home, though, Karla. He's there a lot."

Karla turned to face her visitor. "Bridget, men can't be expected to be mothers. The poor man has to work, too. It's not fair to him that he has to get the dinner and muddle through homework as well. She should not have had children if she was not willing to raise them."

Bridget remained silent, conscious of the clear windows in the glass house in which she sat.

Karla, no doubt considering the feelings of her visitor, continued to talk. "I know you work but you make sure your children are seen to. And you cook and do their homework with them. Don't deny it, Bridget, I've seen you doing homework with your kids."

Bridget, comfortably back in the virtuous camp, nodded, as if she had just been caught at something. "It's true. I do, Karla. I have to admit that I don't think it's fair for a man to have to do everything."

"I agree," Karla answered, relieved. "That's probably why there are so many divorces."

"No doubt."

The women silently considered the state of the world.

"Bridget, were you at early Mass last week?"

Bridget nodded.

"Did you get a look at the new priest?"

"I did, Karla. He looks nice."

"Looks can be deceiving, though, can't they?" Karla answered with a secretive look. "I heard that there was trouble in his last parish."

Bridget eyes widened. "What kind of trouble?"

"I heard it was something to do with a woman. And the parish finance committee."

"Was he involved with the woman?"

"I don't know for sure, Bridget. You know me. I don't like to gossip so I'll not say anything else but there was talk."

The two exchanged knowing looks.

"You're right not to gossip, Karla."

"I'm just not like that, Bridget. Did you see his car?"

"No. Is it nice?"

"My husband said it cost $30,000 if it cost a penny."

"Do they get paid that much?"

"Maybe if they're in charge of the parish finances."

Bridget said nothing and Karla changed the subject. "We'll have to keep our eyes open. I told my husband that it was no good expecting everyone else to do the work. We try to stay active in the parish and do our part."

"You do, Karla. You always do your part."

Karla accepted this as her due. "God knows I try, Bridget. I do not shirk my responsibility."

Bridget finished her tea and rose. "I have to go, Karla. Thanks for the chat."

"Most people are too busy to chat anymore. It's sad, isn't it?"

"Yes. It's a sad world."

"We'll see you again, Bridget. God bless."

Jesus looked on as both women returned to their separate lives. His face, serious in the extreme, reflected pain. The Lord's eyes followed Bridget as she got into her car and started the ignition. Jesus stared intently into Bridget's soul for a moment, allowing her to feel His presence.

Bridget completed her evening work mechanically, lost in thought. Feelings of anxiety had annoyed her all afternoon. Something about the conversation with Karla made her feel terribly uncomfortable. Ugh. She tried to shake it off as she peeled potatoes.

Bob, her husband, came in fast and furiously, fifteen minutes before dinner.

"Hi," he greeted her, throwing his coat over a chair and moving toward the door to take a shower. "I have to go out right after dinner. There's a meeting for everyone working on the Spring Committee."

Bridget nodded. She had forgotten about the meeting.

"What's wrong?" he asked, sensing her mood.

"Nothing," she answered slowly. "I don't really know."

He stopped in his tracks. "You don't know?"

Shaking her head, Bridget felt tears burning her eyes. "I don't know."

Bob stepped back into the room, looking at her closely. "You must have some idea, Bridget. What's the matter?"

Bridget put down the potato peeler and moved behind him to close the door. The children listened to every word. "I had an upsetting conversation today. It's got me bothered, that's all."

Bob, noting the closed door, sighed and settled into a chair. This would not be quick. "Who were you talking to?"

"Karla."

He rolled his eyes. "Give me the bad news. Who's sleeping with whom? Who's pregnant? Who's embezzling funds?"

"Stop it, Bob. It's not funny."

"Sorry."

Bridget sat down across from him. "It's upsetting, that's all."

Bob nodded. "We've established that. What part of the conversation upset you? Help me out here, Bridget."

"Bob, do you ever think about God?"

"What?"

"Do you ever think about God?"

"Bridget, what the heck are you talking about? What does this have to do with Karla? Has Karla converted to Buddhism or something?"

Bridget answered slowly. "No. On the contrary. Karla never misses Mass and she does her part in the community and in the parish. For all the world understands, Karla is a saint."

Her husband's face became serious. "That's how it looks, Bridget, but it takes more than going to Mass to be a saint."

Bridget began to cry.

"What happened?" her husband demanded. "Why are you crying?"

"I'm crying because she's such a mean witch. It's so ugly, Bob. Every time I talk to her she tears people to shreds. You know the new priest? She said there was talk that he stole money, either with a woman, from a woman, or because of a woman. She implied awful things. She talked about Agnes Worthington." Bridget paused. "She's pregnant, by the way."

Bob nodded. "Somebody usually is."

"There's a new child in the school and his mother is from the city. She was cruel about her. I mean, cruel, saying this woman didn't cook and had beer in her refrigerator." Bridget began to cry again. "I should have gotten up and walked out, Bob. I should have. But I didn't. I sat there and let her go on about all these people and actually agreed with her about some of it. If you don't agree with her you get the feeling she'll start tearing you to shreds. I feel like I need a shower."

Bob understood. "She's a gossip, Bridget. Don't go over there. She's poison, no matter how many committees she's on or how often she goes to Mass. And she can cook all she wants, but she sets a terrible example for her kids because she never has a nice thing to say about anyone. Now, is that all?"

"I feel like I'm a big disappointment to God."

"Ah. The God part," Bob observed. "How does God come into it?"

"You're going to think I'm crazy."

"I always think you're crazy. What does God have to do with Karla?"

"Bob, I felt like He was there. When I got into my car I was upset and I felt like He was looking at me, you know, disappointed about the conversation. It made me feel terrible."

Bob remained silent.

"I don't think it's okay to talk like that about people."

"It's not okay, Bridget. You know that. Why would I think you're crazy?"

"It was a strong feeling, Bob. I haven't been right all

afternoon."

Bob looked out the window, considering. "We go to Mass. We say our prayers. And we're supposed to be nice. God doesn't like that gossipy stuff. It makes sense to me, Bridget. He was there and He was disappointed. But you're not like that. Confess it next time you go to Confession. Then promise God you'll stop upsetting your husband and that you'll give him whatever he wants."

Bridget nodded thoughtfully. "I will…tell it in Confession, that is. I'm not like that and I'm not going to pretend I'm like that to keep her happy. Next time I'll say, 'Karla, that woman is raising a child by herself. The last thing she needs is us talking about her.' And if she says one more thing about the priest I'll tell her to shove it."

Bob's eyes lit up. "That's my girl. Tell her to shove it. God would like that. You said you needed a shower. Come and take a shower with me."

She laughed and picked up her potato peeler. "I don't think so."

The Report Card

With shaking hands, Julie's mother replaced the report card in the glove compartment of her daughter's car. Olivia's worst fears were now confirmed. Julie had been lying about school and heaven knew what else. Behind the report card was a small folded piece of newspaper with white powder in it. Olivia put it in her pocket.

"Did you find the glasses?" asked her husband.

"No," she replied. Olivia got out of the car and looked at her husband Daniel waiting by their car. Julie, their twenty-two year old daughter, often borrowed sunglasses and kept them. Daniel's were missing. Olivia decided not to tell him about the failed courses and the envelope.

"They're not here. Check the floor under your seat."

That afternoon, Julie came down from her bedroom into the kitchen.

"Good morning," her mother greeted her. "You're sleeping late these days."

Julie grunted and Olivia studied her as she put two pieces of bread in the toaster. At five foot six, Julie usually weighed about 135 pounds. In the last six months, Olivia noticed her weight dropping. She looked gaunt, her mother noted. There were dark circles under her eyes and she kept odd hours, often sleeping in until early afternoon. Olivia stared at her daughter with a newly acquired clarity. The thought in her head crystallized with appalling suddenness. Julie was not just using drugs. She was addicted to them.

"What did you do last night?"

Julie frowned. Her once clear, bright eyes closed

momentarily. "I went to the movies with Dawn. Afterwards we got pizza."

Olivia nodded but did not respond. Dawn had called looking for her at eleven p.m. Lies rolled off her daughter's tongue.

"No classes today?"

"No. It's a staff day."

More lies.

"Julie, sit down with me. We need to talk."

Julie frowned and pushed unruly hair back from her face. Looking at her mother with distaste, she spoke groggily. "Mom, I don't want to talk. I have cramps, okay?"

"I want to talk, Julie. And I want to talk now."

Julie dropped into a chair opposite her and stared vacantly at Olivia.

"What?"

"Julie, where are all of your friends? Why don't you see them anymore? The only ones who call here are the people from the restaurant."

Julie had begun a waitress job a year ago. Her new companions were troubled and Olivia knew it. The problem was that all of Julie's nice friends seemed to have fallen away.

"Mom, I can't go to school and work and still keep up with a million friends. Why are you doing this to me? I'm tired."

"Why are you so tired?" Olivia inquired.

"It's morning and I just got up. Give me a break."

Olivia looked pointedly at the clock above her daughter's head. "It's 2 in the afternoon, Julie."

Julie looked confused and turned to check the clock herself. "Oh wow. I didn't know it was that late. It's because of the cramps, I guess."

Olivia prayed for guidance. "You look terrible. You've lost weight. There are dark circles under your eyes. And Julie, I know about school."

"What about school?"

"You failed all but one of your classes. You told me you had a B average. Julie, you lie about everything. I found this in your glove compartment."

The small packet of newspaper found its way to the table. Julie stood up abruptly and began to shout. "How dare you spy on me! My grades are my business. You have no idea the pressure I'm under. That is not mine. I don't know where you found it in your covert investigating, but it's not mine."

Olivia, startled at her daughter's violent response, held her ground. "We're helping you pay for school so it is our business. I was looking for your father's sunglasses. If it's not yours, whose is it?"

"How do I know? Maybe I should just move out. You wouldn't care. All you care about is your stupid gardening club." Julie, once so sweet, looked at her mother with hatred. "You don't know anything about how hard it is. You just nag and criticize. Why should I work so hard for grades? You're the one who wants me to go to college. It's not your life, Mother. It's mine. Stay out of it and mind your own damn business."

Julie stormed from the room and slammed the door so hard Olivia thought it would break. She took a deep breath and tried to calm her panic. She would remember this day, she knew. It was the day her denial ended.

Olivia took an envelope from her purse and laid it on the counter by her daughter's backpack. In it was a statement from a bank who had apparently given Julie a $10,000 student loan six months ago. Olivia and Daniel had paid for all of their daughter's fees. She had no living expenses and she worked nearly full-time. Where had all of that money gone? Just a few days ago Julie asked her for gas money to get to work. Olivia knew that her daughter would see the envelope and know that Olivia knew about the loan. That was what she wanted. The truth had to be faced.

They had seen the changes in their daughter, of course. The once cheerful young woman had become surly and inconsistent. One day she would be bubbly and energetic, the next tense and withdrawn. She slept a lot when she was home, which was seldom. Olivia sometimes wondered if her daughter worked as much as she said she did as there were several occasions when she was supposed to be at work and the restaurant had called looking for her. The most damning evidence was the report card, of course. Julie had gotten no credits at all this semester and Olivia guessed she had not even attended the courses. How could they have been so blind?

Olivia stayed at the table and prayed for guidance. They needed help, she thought suddenly, professional help. Searching through the yellow pages, she looked up drug addiction and dialed the number for Narcotics Anonymous. Forty-five minutes later, she felt clear-sighted and determined, if heartbroken. She picked up the phone to call her husband at work and ruin his day.

Olivia's guardian angel prayed silently as Olivia spoke to her husband. A heavenly resident appeared, St. Daniel Camboni, and conferred with the angel in answer to Olivia's prayers.

"It won't happen immediately," St. Daniel informed the angel. "Julie is not willing to stop. Let's pray that God fill the parents with hope and trust. We'll protect their daughter as best we can until the time is right. In the meantime, the counselor will help them to cope."

The angel understood. It was often the case that a soul persisted in error. The trust, hope and prayers of loved ones often provided graces for protection until such a time as the soul was ready to change. Feeling confident that a good outcome would eventually be obtained, Olivia's angel prayed earnestly for the mother's peace.

Six months later, the phone rang at midnight. Olivia rolled over in bed and fumbled for it in the darkness. A nearby hospital informed her that her daughter had been in a car accident and was in the emergency room.

"Daniel," Olivia said in a tight voice. "Daniel, wake up. We have to go."

They drove to the hospital in silence. Conversation seemed pointless. Each muttered their own fearful prayers. Julie had deteriorated before their eyes in the last six months. There was no pretense of school anymore. She no longer explained where she went or bothered to make up lies. Daniel and Olivia had recently discussed asking her to leave but feared for her safety. A substance abuse counselor explained that until Julie was ready to quit doing drugs, they could not help her. They begged Julie to enter a rehabilitation program but she refused, insisting that she did not have a problem. Olivia simply prayed and hoped that her daughter would not die.

The busyness of the emergency room contrasted to the quiet night streets and Olivia and Daniel blinked at the lights and activity. Following signs, they went to reception and asked for their daughter. A nurse brought them back to a cubicle in the corner of a filled ward.

Olivia reacted in anguish at the sight of her only child. A bandage wrapped around her daughter's head showed evidence of blood staining. A tube led from Julie's mouth to a machine that rose and fell, breathing for Julie. The rest of her body was covered in a sheet. A doctor came in right behind them and began to explain the extent of the injuries. "Your daughter has suffered a head injury," he began. "She was thrown from a car. She has some broken bones in her legs, but her spine is fine. We're concerned about swelling in her brain and for that reason we have given her a drug that paralyzes her. This is to protect her while we assess the injury."

The doctor went on, explaining that the initial twelve hours were critical. Olivia felt no tears. Hadn't they known something would happen? She now prayed as hard as she had ever prayed in her life.

"God, protect my daughter's soul," she begged. Julie had not gone to Mass or Confession in years, she knew. What if she died in this condition?

"We need a priest," she burst out, interrupting the doctor, who continued to explain the medical situation. "Julie should have a priest."

The doctor nodded. "Your daughter was given Last Rites shortly after she arrived. She was wearing a Scapular so we called the Chaplain. He'll be in to talk to you."

Olivia began to cry then. Julie had scoffed at the brown Scapular when Olivia offered it to her two weeks before. It had been left on the counter. Determined, Olivia had placed it on her daughter's dresser. Julie must have put it on.

Surely heaven would care for her daughter, Olivia thought. Wasn't this just the kind of situation heaven wanted to help with? The fact that Julie was wearing the Scapular told her a lot about her little girl's soul. Suddenly, Olivia knew that Julie would be all right.

Left with their daughter, Olivia assured her husband.

"She'll be fine, Daniel. She'll change now."

Three guardian angels prayed with Olivia and Daniel in the little cubicle. Our Lady appeared and began to pray with them, thanking God for protecting Julie in the accident and asking that God surround her in grace while she recovered. The angels felt great joy. They knew that Our Lady's prayers obtained stunning results.

"She will learn to love God during her convalescence," Mary assured the angels. "Bring the counselor I have chosen to her next week and all will be well."

The following week, Julie rested comfortably in a hospital room. Her legs were encased in plaster casts, as well as one of her arms. The head injury had been surprisingly mild but a seizure necessitated medication. Olivia sat in a chair next to the bed, holding her daughter's hand.

"I'm tired, Mom," Julie said.

"It's the medication," Olivia answered.

Julie sighed. "No, Mom. I mean I'm really tired. I'm tired of my life."

Olivia remained silent.

"I've been so terrible." Julie began to cry. "I want help. I want to talk to someone. I am doing drugs. I was messed up the night of the accident. I'm so sorry, Mom. Please help me."

Olivia put her arms around her daughter and rocked her back and forth. "We'll get you the right help, Julie. We have the nicest counselor. She used to use drugs a long time ago and she got better. Dad and I have talked to her twice this week. She'll come up here and see you. This happens to lots of people and they get better. You'll get better, too. Don't be afraid. We love you and we'll help you."

Daniel came in and Olivia looked up at her husband in joy. "Julie wants help."

A Night Out

"Are you coming out tonight?"

Linda shook her head. "Mark is on the road and I can't get a babysitter."

"I have a couple of names if you want them," offered Sue, another nurse on the cancer ward. "I can make a couple of calls for you."

Linda shook her head again and continued her chart work. "I'm kind of tired anyway, Sue. I'm going to pass tonight."

Sue organized her injections and left the nurses station with a pitying look. "You'll miss all the fun. Bill the accountant will be looking for you."

"He'll live," Linda guessed.

Linda considered her friends as she finished her work. Thursday nights out with the girls were fun, it was true. But lately Linda had been evaluating everything, including her marriage. Some of the Thursday night 'fun' would prompt a woman to evaluate her marriage.

The nurses went to a local bar that offered two for one drinks for ladies on Thursday nights. These evenings began as low key sessions but had taken a turn recently.

Linda recalled the events of the previous Thursday and felt her face grow red. After an hour of drinking, one of the girls had ordered shots of tequila to celebrate Linda's birthday. Feeling compelled to accept, Linda drank the shot, along with another one besides. One of the nurses then introduced Linda to her brother, an accountant named Bill. What followed was hazy. Linda knew they talked and danced and had a vague recollection of him asking her to dinner before she left. He knew she was married, of course. Linda never hid the fact that she was married. Bill was funny and entertaining, but what kind of a man asked a married woman out to dinner?

The nurses teased Linda all week and Bill's sister encouraged her to meet him again, calling the evening harmless fun. Linda wasn't so sure.

Mark, her husband, drove a truck over the road, which meant that he was away two nights a week. Their eight-year marriage was fine. There was nothing wrong with it that Linda could see. Mark was a good father to their two children. He was a good husband. Linda trusted him. Maybe she was bored.

All week she kept thinking of how she would feel if Mark were behaving in the same way and she knew she would not like it at all. Whatever was happening, Thursday nights weren't going to improve the situation. Linda had liked Bill the accountant. That made her nervous.

She sighed as she finished her paperwork and closed the files.

Linda's guardian angel prayed, thanking God that Linda had resisted the temptation to go out. Linda was in danger and her guardian angel knew it. Her companions were encouraging her to take the first steps down a path that led away from her husband and marriage. Heaven's angel had whispered constantly to Linda all week, helping her to understand the peril in what others called innocent fun. He understood what Linda did not. The future of her family was at stake.

Mark drove without thinking, as he so often did. He liked his job. It was clear and understandable. He took a load of construction materials from one place to another so that others could build houses for families. He liked the predictability of it all. The trip could change, of course, according to weather and road conditions, but for the most part he knew where he would be on any given day and he found this to be good.

This day was like most other days except for one thing. When Mark stopped at his usual Friday lunch spot, the parking lot was filled. He managed to find a place for the truck, but it meant he could not lay out his newspaper and read in his usual booth. He spotted some truckers he knew and joined them.

"What's happening?" Mark asked one of the men at the table.

"Funeral," answered the other trucker. "Big deal around here. The mayor of the town lost his daughter in a car accident."

"Too bad," Mark replied. "Young girl?"

"Thirty-two," informed the man. "Two small kids. She was a nurse."

Mark looked around at the crowded room. His wife Linda was a thirty-two year old nurse with two children. Hmm. Some coincidence.

Mark walked to the bathroom after ordering and glanced into the main restaurant. He saw the mayor, whom he recognized, along with the mayor's wife. Also at their table was a man near Mark's age. A small girl of about five years old lay in his lap with her head on his shoulder. The guy looked like he had been banged with a wood plank and Mark knew immediately that this was the widower. He looked quickly away.

Back on the road, Mark tried to shake off a feeling of heaviness. He could not forget the look on that guy's face.

What would you tell a five-year-old girl? Your mother is never coming back?

Mark shook his head with a deep frown. People got over it. They had to. But man, he wouldn't wish that kind of pain on anyone.

He considered his own wife and children. At four and three, the kids were a handful. Very often he arrived home and Linda headed out the door to work. Their house was all about the kids right now. Linda worked three nights a week and he was gone two nights a week. It seemed to Mark sometimes that his life was a revolving door of work and kids, work and kids. He thought about his wife.

Linda seemed happy enough. She was cheerful. Lately, though, Mark sensed a restlessness in her. Something seemed to be on her mind. Mark figured it would pass and he never brought it up. Driving home on this Friday, though, he thought about the guy back in the restaurant and decided that maybe he'd better ask her about it. He picked up his phone to call home.

Mark's guardian angel closed his eyes in petition as he begged heaven for graces. When Mark picked up the cell phone, the angel relaxed.

"Hello," Linda answered.

"It's me," Mark said. "How are things?"

"Good. Everything's fine."

"How are the kids?"

Linda surveyed their children in the dishevelled living room. It would take thirty minutes to clean it. "Good. They're good."

"What's up with you?"

"Nothing."

"Did you go out last night?"

"No. I was tired. I came home."

"Are you sick?"

Linda raised her eyebrows. "I'm fine, Mark. What's wrong?"

Silence followed.

"Mark, what's wrong?"

"I don't know. I'm wondering if you're okay, that's all. You seem…unhappy lately."

Linda closed her eyes. Something like relief swelled in her. Perhaps it was because Mark had cared enough to ask. "I'm not unhappy. But I feel like you and I are disconnected. We never seem to talk."

"I know. We're busy. Let's go out by ourselves tonight."

"We'd have to get a babysitter," Linda warned. Money was tight.

"Then we have to get a babysitter. Let's do it, Linda. We need to get out. I feel like all we do is work and I don't mind work but we need to get out."

"Okay. I'll find someone to watch the kids."

Linda hung up the phone feeling lighter and more cheerful than she had in ages. A quick phone call secured a sitter and she thought about where they would go and what she would wear. It would be fun to go out with Mark. They used to go out every Friday night. Linda thought about last Friday and how she had felt after the night out with the girls. She shuddered.

Thank God I came home last night, she thought in relief. Imagine if I had been out until two a.m. talking to Bill again. Linda cleaned the living room in deep thought. She knew she would not go out on Thursday nights anymore.

A Bad Week

Father Damien drove with one hand on the steering wheel and the other out the window. The resistance of the wind against his hand provided his inner turmoil with a distracting physical sensation on which to concentrate. Everything seemed upside down. Damien could not determine if it was his head or heart, or maybe his soul, which suffered such distress. One thing was certain. Things were not going well.

Yesterday one of his counseling clients died of an overdose. She had been drug-free for two years. Last week there had been a suicide in one of the families he counseled. Before that a young pregnant woman he worked with had opted for an abortion. This morning he had been verbally attacked by a parishioner after Mass.

Ten years ago Father Damien celebrated his ordination. Certainty of his vocation remained with him during the last ten years. Trained as a substance abuse counselor, Damien worked with a treatment center and was attached to a parish, but the certainty he felt in his vocation had recently vanished. In its place were doubts, fears, insecurities, anger, and disillusionment. The very souls he tried to minister to attacked him. The Church seemed inconsistent in that his Bishop ignored Rome's directives and even ridiculed priests Damien respected. Some priests he knew seemed faithful. Others were cynical and bitter. The diocese continued to reel from revelations of sexual abuse by priests and Damien felt sickened.

"What's the point?" he asked himself.

He considered his destination. He was going on retreat to a Franciscan Monastery with a short stop first at an old friend's. He felt the need to have his Confession heard. Maybe he would ask his friend to hear it. The retreat was a must right now. Any more dead clients or aggressive parishioners and he would snap.

Damien wondered, not for the first time, whether the solitude and peace of a monastery would be more in keeping with his vocation. Something had to change and he felt drawn to the quiet. Yes, the peace drew him like a magnet. Compared to the mess of the world, the monastic life stood out like a pristine example of heavenly calm and order.

Before noon, Damien pulled into the driveway of Father Tom's parish house. Tom Bailey had been at the seminary with Damien and Damien respected him. Their paths seldom crossed these days but Damien knew he could speak freely about his struggles. Tom was discreet.

The doorbell brought no response and Damien lifted up the potted plant at the bottom of the stairs. Finding the key, he let himself in. By the time Tom arrived back, he was drinking a cup of coffee with his feet up.

"Sorry I wasn't here," Tom greeted him. Dressed in jeans and sport shirt, Tom looked tanned and healthy. Damien considered himself and how frumpy he looked. He wore his collar and needed new clothes badly. He kept meaning to go shopping.

"You look great," he told Tom. "Where did you get the tan?"

"Vacation," Tom reported. "You should try it sometime."

Damien sighed. "I need the break. That's for sure."

"How's it going?"

Damien sighed. "Great. Bodies are piling up all around me and my parishioners hate me."

Tom laughed. "Nice. You're knocking them dead, eh?"

Damien laughed in spite of himself. "It would seem that

way. I'm burned out, I guess. What do you make of Barry Wexley?"

Father Barry Wexley was the latest pedophile to be accused in their diocese.

Tom rummaged through the kitchen, making sandwiches. "Are you hungry?" Damien nodded.

"I don't make anything of it. He's a sick son of a gun and he always was. Damien, do you remember him in the seminary? He hung out in strange places. That was a tip and a clue."

Damien agreed. "It was clear something was wrong."

"It's not my problem," Tom insisted. "I'm not going to get drawn into this mess. The Bishop can handle it."

"He says all the right things," Damien said thoughtfully.

"He's a political animal," Tom replied. "He knows what he's doing in that respect."

Damien took this silently. Should the Bishop be a political animal?

"Trust me," Tom continued as he put a plate of sandwiches down. "The Bishop will come out all right. He's savvy."

"I got nailed for him in front of church this morning," Damien told him. "One of the old ladies told me off. She says the Bishop is in disobedience to the Holy Father because he is on a committee to explore the ordination of women."

"And this is your fault?"

"Yep. And she 'has her doubts' about me."

Tom laughed aloud. "What did she mean?"

Damien took a sandwich and stared at it. "I don't know. It could be the Barry Wexley thing. It could be the Bishop's public stance against the Vatican. I don't know. Through the grace of God, we were interrupted."

"God can be helpful that way. Damien, what do you care what some old lady thinks?"

Damien considered. "She's a good woman, Tom. In Mass every day, says the Rosary…"

Tom raised his hand. "Say no more. I know the type. Stay away from them. They'll drive you batty."

Damien laughed. "I can't stay away from them. They're my parishioners. They're in Confession every weekend."

Tom shook his head. "You're a fool, buddy. I have Confessions by appointment."

"What? You don't have them every weekend?"

"No way. It's a waste of time. Same people every week, confessing the same stuff. What's the point?"

Damien struggled. A bad feeling found a spot in his stomach. "Tom, the parish is supposed to offer Confessions."

"I do. If they want me to hear their Confession, all they have to do is call."

"But you're never home," Damien noted.

"I have an answering machine." Tom ate his sandwich, giving Damien a defiant look. "You're letting these people run your life."

Damien felt a mist around him. "Tom, they're my parishioners. It's my job, I think."

"You're taking it too seriously, buddy. I can see it in your face."

Damien chewed thoughtfully, resolving not to ask his friend to hear his Confession.

"One of my clients overdosed last week."

Tom put his sandwich down. "Bad luck, man. But that's going to happen."

"That's true. I know that. But she was doing so well. She had come so far, Tom. I saw her three days before and she seemed fine but I could have missed something."

Tom rolled his eyes. "Damien, what can you do? A certain percentage of drug users will die from drugs. Shake it off."

"You're right. I know you're right. Her name was Margaret."

"Who else died?"

"A young boy, twenty-one. Suicide. His father is a recovering alcoholic." Damien's face reflected his pain. "I did family counseling with them. I didn't see it. I knew he was depressed. I talked to him about it. But I didn't see it coming."

"That makes it your fault then. Who else?"

Damien frowned, trying to get a handle on his pain. "A baby. A girl came to me, pregnant. The father left. She's seventeen. I tried to connect her with the Crisis Pregnancy people but she decided to abort the baby."

Tom put his sandwich down. "What a week. Damien, people are screwed up. It's not our fault. You can't take this stuff so seriously. If someone wants to use drugs, he's going to use drugs. I shouldn't have to tell you that. And if someone is going to kill himself, nobody can stop him. And if the girl didn't want to keep the baby, what can you do about it? You can't force her to keep it."

Damien, also ignoring his lunch, mused aloud. "I know. But if I were more effective, maybe these deaths could have been prevented."

Tom picked up his sandwich in disgust. "You're too serious. You always were. Shake it off and get on with it. Cut your hours. Have a little fun. Come on vacation with me and lighten up. I'm going away next month for a week."

"Are you going on the diocesan pilgrimage?"

Tom laughed. "You must be joking. Wild horses couldn't get me on that pilgrimage. I'm going to the beach. Come with me. You need the break. You can't be a priest 24/7. You're burning yourself out and you can't help anyone like this."

Damien ate his lunch while Tom talked. They discussed the Church's position on celibacy and the ordination of women. Tom felt both changes were coming and who was he to stand in the way of progress? He also warned Damien that the Bishop did not look favorably on the pro-life movement.

"Is the Bishop pro-choice?" Damien asked, appalled.

"Let's just say he's on the fence," Tom informed him. "He had a run-in with a priest in the city about speaking out with the pro-lifers."

"Not Francis Hennigan?"

Tom nodded.

Damien had the greatest respect for Francis Hennigan. All week he had determined to phone him, offering support, but the parish tragedies had taken over. "How can the Bishop be against pro-lifers?" Damien asked. He was beginning to feel sorry he had stopped at all.

"He's not against them. He just thinks they're over the top," Tom replied soothingly. "Let the courts decide, keep Church and state separate, all that stuff. Damien, can I give you a piece of advice?"

Damien, still thinking of Francis Hennigan, nodded.

"Lighten up. You're not going to get anywhere in this diocese if you don't relax. Keep your head down and do your job. That's what I'm doing and the Bishop loves me."

Damien looked at his friend across the table. His confusion mounted. "You think so?"

"I know so. Stay out of the line of fire. You've got a great future but if you go in for this pro-life business you'll make enemies."

"Francis Hennigan sure has," Damien said thoughtfully. "You know, Tom, Christ had enemies."

"Yeah? Well, Christ needs to police his Bishops. I'm not going to get into a match with this guy about things that are not my problem. I'm giving you good advice. Stay out of it. Let Hennigan fight his own battles. He's going to hang himself with all those Rosaries. Promise me you'll come on vacation with me next month and we'll fight all this out over drinks."

Damien rose. "I promise you I'll think about it."

"I'll have to be satisfied with that, I guess. It's great to see you, Damien."

"You, too, Tom. Thanks for listening."

Damien's guardian angel prayed passionately. Considering the situation, the angel called upon St. Damien, who came at once.

"He went seeking bread and was given a stone," the angel lamented.

St. Damien looked at the priest with compassion.

"We cannot deny him the battle, dear angel, because it is through the battle he will be purified. He is learning to be a fool for Christ. Have no fear. Help is coming."

Damien drove automatically, his mind far away. The words and faces of the week swirled through his mind in racing thoughts. Tom's words particularly affected him. Was Damien too serious? Could a person be too serious about working with God's people?

Tom warned him to stay away from Francis Hennigan. Damien frowned in confusion. Francis Hennigan was a holy man, perhaps the holiest man Damien had ever met. Wasn't this working against God's goals? Did the Church not have a duty to support God's will in the world? What about justice? Everyone talked about justice. Where was the justice in abortion, Damien wondered?

"Lighten up," he heard Tom saying. Damien felt again as

though he had been kicked in the stomach.

I should quit, he thought suddenly. I should leave the priesthood. I'm not good at it. I'm not helping anyone. My parishioners are killing themselves and each other with my help. I've got it all wrong. Tom is relaxed. Tom looks good. I'm a mess. I could start a private practice. Or teach. I could teach. I should skip this retreat and look for apartments near the college campus.

For the next three hours Damien wrestled with tumultuous thoughts. Try as he might, he could not escape his distress. It felt as though he were tumbling around in a clothes dryer.

Mentally exhausted and spiritually depleted, Damien arrived at the monastery and parked. Grabbing his overnight bag, he crossed the parking lot with a gait as fast as his thoughts. Inside, he dropped to his knees near the front of the empty church and put his head in his hands.

"God, God. Can You hear me? I need help. I need help now, God."

After a momentary silence, a creaking sound heralded the arrival of someone through the sacristy. Damien lifted his head and heard a slow shuffle. An old priest in a brown robe moved slowly toward the tabernacle. The man leaned against the altar and genuflected reverently, with apparent pain.

Arthritis, Damien thought.

The priest came toward him. Damien noted the peaceful countenance and compared it to Tom's intensity. This man's eyes were deeply lined with time. Wisdom and kindness seemed to flow out from him and Damien felt comforted by his mere presence.

"Father Damien?" asked the old priest.

"Yes, Father. I'm Damien."

"You're late," he said pleasantly.

"I stopped on the way. Are you Father Kevin?"

"Guilty of that and much more, I'm afraid. Welcome."

Father Kevin offered his hand and Damien rose and shook it. He looked into the older man's eyes and burst out, "I'm in trouble, Father Kevin. I'm thinking of quitting the priesthood."

Father Kevin nodded. "I see. Jesus has no further use for you?"

Damien frowned. "Uh…I don't know. I didn't think of that. It's just that I'm not very good at being a priest. I'm afraid I'm doing damage."

Kevin's kind eyes held the younger priest's gaze. "Perhaps you should let Christ be the priest. Christ never does damage."

"I'm confused."

"I see that," Father Kevin said, with a touch of humor in his voice. He picked up Damien's bag and placed his arm on Damien's shoulder. "You've come to the right place. Jesus is here. Jesus will restore you. Let me take you to your room."

A burden lifted from Damien's shoulders as he allowed Father Kevin to lead him. His mind slowed a bit. Gentleness descended upon him. He felt as though he had run a hard race.

"Thank God I'm here."

"Yes," Father Kevin answered calmly. "Thank God."

After three days of near silence and frequent Eucharistic Adoration, Father Damien sat with Father Kevin in the mild evening sunshine. The mature and glorious garden of the monastery delighted Damien. Their chairs rocked back and forth and they spoke quietly.

"I don't understand," Damien said. "What was the point of my involvement in these lives if not to positively affect the outcome?"

Father Kevin, all patience, answered quietly. "You are making two mistakes in this situation. The first is that you are assuming the Lord's plan is the same as yours. Damien, only the Lord knows what He willed for these souls. You cannot see the benefit of your involvement because the Lord has no need to show you. Christ wanted to be in these situations so He sent you. Christ was there, Damien. Have no doubt of that. The second mistake you are making is to assume that your job ended with these deaths."

Father Kevin's brown robe matched his eyes, Damien noted, as the older priest looked seriously at him.

"Isn't it more likely that the Lord placed you in that family to minister to them in the tragedy of their son's death? Isn't it also likely that the Lord knew this young girl would choose abortion? Damien, you must not abandon that poor little thing. She will need healing. Who will help her when nobody knows about her situation but you? Your priestly ministering is just beginning in both of these situations."

Father Kevin stopped rocking for a moment.

"The woman who took an overdose causes you sorrow, I know, but she is with her Savior. Do you think Jesus will ignore her valiant effort to become free of the addiction? Damien, Damien, you must work in the light of God's mercy. This light must shine on everything you do. If you see God's mercy all around you, there will be joy. If you lose your joy, you must run immediately to the Source of all joy so that He can replenish it. You cannot give what you do not have and God wants to flow joy to His people."

Damien nodded. His joy had returned here and he thanked God for it. After a long silence, Damien spoke.

"Father Kevin, I don't know if I want to work in the world anymore. I think I might like the contemplative life."

Father Kevin rocked and considered. "Where does Jesus want you, my friend?"

Damien closed his eyes for a moment and thought of his clients and parishioners. Surprisingly, he thought of Francis Hennigan and knew, as much as he knew anything, that Jesus wanted him to help the pro-life priest.

"Jesus wants me to stay where I am and support Francis Hennigan."

Kevin nodded as though this had been obvious to him. "We'll be here, Damien. You can come back to us when you need rest and renewal. I'll pray for you each day, that God will give you the courage to be the priest He needs. Damien, you must measure your priesthood against the Divine Priest. No other."

Damien squinted up into the sun and thought of Tom's tan. "I've been asked to go to the beach next month for a week. It'll be a party."

Kevin remained silent.

"I don't think I will. Being with Tom didn't leave me peaceful."

Kevin spoke. "A priest looking for nourishment should not seek it in the world. The world will feed the priest what the world offers. It can do nothing else. This doesn't benefit the priest. How could it? A priest seeking nourishment, particularly one called to work in the world, must turn his back on the world and seek nourishment from heaven. A man cannot serve two masters. A slave on a journey does not abandon his master simply because he needs rest. The slave rests when the master rests and a priest should rest with Christ, not the enemy of Christ. Seek holy companions, my friend, and you will keep your joy."

"Father Kevin, Tom is a good guy," Damien said, a little confused. "He's a good priest."

"Yes, and you are both acting in obedience to your bishop. But should you follow the path that Christ has marked out for Tom, my friend? Or should you follow the path that Christ has marked out for you?"

Damien felt the last cobwebs of confusion blow away in that garden. Francis Hennigan needed support and if this made Damien unpopular, then so be it. Damien let out a peaceful sigh and leaned back in his rocking chair. He would phone Francis Hennigan this night.

"I don't think I'm going to advance in the diocese," he noted idly.

After a moment of silence, both priests burst out laughing.

The May Crowning

Nora and Andrea worked intently in the fading afternoon sun. Humid, warm air made for sticky working conditions but the seven-year olds barely noticed. Nora picked the flowers and Andrea arranged them in wreathes and bracelets and necklaces. The girls were planning a May Crowning in Nora's backyard because this was the first of May. Nora's older sister was crowning the Blessed Mother at school today. Nora was not allowed to attend so she decided to have her own May Crowning. Her next door neighbor and friend, Andrea, had been conscripted to assist.

"Why do we have to crown Mary?" asked Andrea.

Nora wiped the sweat from her forehead, leaving a streak of dirt across her face. "Because she's the Mother of God. You know…Jesus."

"Who's Jesus?"

"Jesus is God. The Guy who died on the cross."

Andrea nodded but Nora sensed her friend's lack of understanding and attempted to clarify. "Jesus died on the cross because of our sins."

"What's a sin?"

Andrea stood over Nora holding a bunch of lilacs. Nora looked up at her friend and gave a deep sigh. Reaching up, she pulled her friend down next to her on the grass.

"You better sit down and help me braid these flowers. I'll tell you all about it."

Nora, not known for shyness, loved nothing better than an opportunity to chatter.

"Jesus was God. He still is, I think. But now He's God in heaven. When Mary was alive, He came down from heaven and got Himself into Mary's stomach."

Andrea nodded. This was remedial. "Did He come out looking like a baby?"

"Yes," Nora said in relief, glad that Andrea had at least that much knowledge. "He looked like a regular baby. But He was secretly God in disguise. Mary was a nice mom and took care of Him. She was married to Joseph, who got to be the dad."

"Is that why everyone has statues of Mary in their front yards?"

"Yes."

Andrea frowned and Nora sensed a question.

"Why aren't there statues of Joseph?"

Nora rolled her eyes. "Andrea, Joseph just pulled the donkey."

"What donkey?"

Nora began to twist her pigtail. Clearly, this was a bigger job than she anticipated.

"The Christmas donkey."

A light of understanding dawned in Andrea's eyes. "Is this the story about the pregnant lady on a horse in the winter?"

Nora, trying not to be patronizing, nodded. "Yes. That's the one. Only it was a donkey, not a horse. And it was winter, but they didn't have any snow I don't think. They had lots of stars and plenty of diapers in the suitcase."

"She had a Baby in the manger," Andrea continued, eager to show off her newly recalled knowledge.

"That's exactly right," Nora encouraged her. "You're very good at these stories. Now I'll tell you the rest of it. Mary had a real hard time being God's mother. People were terrible to Jesus, Who kept being her Son even after He grew up. Some really bad people nailed Him to a cross. He died there and Mary was just sick about it."

Andrea nodded, wide-eyed. "Who wouldn't be?"

Nora agreed and continued. "Here is the tricky part. He died for us so we have to be good."

Andrea's blue eyes reflected the gravity of the discussion. "Why did He do that for us? He doesn't even know me."

"Andrea, He does too know you. He's God. He knows everything."

"I wonder if He likes me," Andrea reflected, looking down at the flowers in her smudged little hands.

Nora rolled her eyes. "What's not to like? You're a nice girl. Your hair is real pretty. And you always help your mom with the baby. That's the kind of thing God likes."

Andrea looked encouraged. "I'm okay, I guess."

"Sure you are," Nora said heartily. "Jesus likes us all. About the being good part . . . you're not always going to be good. That's just the way it is with kids."

Andrea's face reflected her relief. "That's true, Nora."

"Yes. But you have to try to be good and when you're bad, you have to say you're sorry. Those are the rules."

"Are there more rules?"

Nora considered. "There might be. But none of them are as important as that one. It's real simple. Try to be good. Say you're sorry when you're bad. Go to heaven when you die."

"What's heaven?"

Nora shook her head impatiently as though she had been getting to that. "Heaven is like..." Nora's little face screwed up in concentration. What had her mother said about heaven? "Heaven is like the playground, only better."

Andrea concentrated. "Where is it?"

Nora pointed up to the sky. "Up there."

Andrea looked up in wonder. "Does everyone get to go?"

"Everyone who loves God."

Andrea smiled. "I think I love God."

"Of course you love God. He's real nice. He loves you. You

love Him. Only bad people don't love God."

"What about people who don't know about God?"

Nora spoke carefully because she did not want to make a mistake. "We have to tell them about God. But if they die and they never knew about God, they can still get into the playground but they have to promise to play nice."

"That's fair," Andrea said. "People should play nice."

"Thomas Farley does not always play nice," Nora observed reflectively.

Andrea's face showed indignation. "You're right, Nora. He doesn't. I hate Thomas Farley."

Nora pounced on this. "You can't hate him, Andrea. I forgot that rule. You can't hate anyone, even if they're mean to you."

"That might be hard, Nora."

"I know," Nora answered, shaking her head in resignation. "It's very hard. Especially when it's your brother or sister you hate."

Andrea looked distressed. This happened regularly in her experience. "What do you do if you hate your brother or sister?"

Nora, wise from previous struggle, answered solemnly. "You say, 'Jesus, take this hate away. Get it out of here, Jesus. Throw it out the window or something.'"

Andrea laughed in delight. "Throw it in the toilet, Jesus."

Nora laughed too. "Flush it away, Jesus."

"Put it out with the garbage, Jesus," Andrea suggested.

"Smash it down with rocks, Jesus," Nora added.

After a good laugh, the girls turned their attention back to the flowers and worked in silence. A drowsy contentment overcame them as the sun moved on in the sky.

"Nora?"

"Yes?"

"What's the sin part?"

"The sin part is the being bad part," Nora said, effortlessly resuming the lecture. "The mistakes. The hating your brothers or sisters. Think of it like anything you did when you felt real mean inside."

"I get it. Like hitting someone or throwing your shoes at someone."

"Right. Just say you're sorry and it's over."

"That's pretty easy," Andrea observed.

"Not when you're mad, it's not," Nora cautioned. "When you're mad it can be hard to say you're sorry. Sometimes it takes awhile."

"That's true," agreed her friend. "Is that okay?"

"Sure," Nora said expansively. "God doesn't mind waiting for awhile as long as it gets done."

Glancing at the fruit of their labor, the girls decided they were ready.

"Now I get to crown Mary, Andrea, because it was my idea."

Andrea nodded her head a little wistfully and Nora felt badly. She remembered how she felt this morning as her mother readied her sister's hair for the special event at school.

"Maybe we should both crown her," Nora suggested. "First I'll crown her and then you crown her and then she'll have two crowns."

"Perfect," Andrea said happily. "What about Jesus? Should we do something for Him, seeing as He died on the cross and all?"

Nora frowned. This was unorthodox. Mary was crowned in May and that was all there was to it. Nora did not like to discourage her friend, though, given the newness of her participation in all of these heavenly things. She thought fast.

"Jesus is King, Andrea. He wears a crown all the time, even on the cross. I'll show you in our hallway. That's where we keep Him on the cross. We can't really keep crowning Him, I don't think." She considered some more. "My mother lights candles for Him but we can't do that without getting in trouble."

"We wouldn't be making a sin if we didn't feel mad inside," Andrea pointed out.

"There's another part to that, Andrea," Nora warned. "You can't do anything you know is wrong, even if you're not mad when you do it. No. We can't crown Jesus. It's just not done in May. I know. We'll make Him a big bouquet of flowers and put it by the Sacred Heart picture."

"What's the Sacred Heart picture?"

Nora let out her breath impatiently. They had to wrap this up.

"It's a picture they took of Jesus when He was having a better day. Sacred means clean and the heart stands for how much He loves us. Now I'll sing the song and you carry the crown and then you sing the song and I'll carry the crown. We have to hurry, Andrea. Catholics don't spend all day at this, you know."

Two days later, Nora looked out her window. Andrea sat alone on her front porch. Nora opened the door and peeked out. It was early in the morning for a visit.

"What are you doing, Andrea?" she asked her friend. "Do you want to come in?"

Andrea shook her head. "We had some bad news, Nora."

"Should I get my mom?"

"No. Come out and play with me."

Nora agreed and went to ask her mother, who gave permission. She sat down on the steps next to Andrea and began the laborious task of putting on her new sandals. The buckles were terribly stiff, but her mother would not let her force her foot in so Nora had to unbuckle and buckle each one.

"What's your bad news?"

Andrea struggled for words and Nora, intrigued, forgot about her sandals.

"What is it?"

"My grandpa died."

Nora, eyes wide, went uncharacteristically speechless.

"He died during the night," Andrea said, sniffling. "My mom and dad are gone to his house. I guess they left in the middle of the night. When I woke up this morning my aunt was there. Nobody told me he was sick, Nora."

Nora listened, staring into her friend's eyes. "You must be very sad. Did you cry?"

Andrea nodded. "I cried and cried."

Nora accepted this as natural and understandable. Hadn't she also cried when her grandpa died?

"Well," Nora said with a deep sigh. "He's in heaven."

Deep lines appeared in Andrea's face. "How do you know, Nora? What if he did not love God? What if he went to hell? Nora, where is hell?"

Nora sat back against the bricks of the wall. Not for a moment did she feel out of her depth. "Hell is under the street. But he did not go to hell."

"He might have. He said bad words all the time."

Nora weighed this judiciously. "My dad says bad words sometimes, too. That doesn't mean he's all bad. You have to be all bad to go to hell."

Andrea had more on her mind. "What happens in hell, Nora? Is it a terrible place?"

"You bet. People get run over by cars down there. It's full of zombies and witches and monsters." Seeing the horror on her friend's face, Nora began to speak quickly. "My mom says we should never worry about hell. She says it's not something little girls need to think about because God is so good that He tries to talk everyone into going to heaven."

Andrea looked comforted and Nora continued.

"My mom says that God is so good at talking people into coming to heaven and playing nice that she thinks there might only be a few people in hell."

"They'd have to have someone to drive the cars," Andrea mused.

"That's true. One or two monsters could do that."

The girls sat, silently considering.

"Nora, I hope my grandpa is in heaven."

"Did they light candles?" Nora asked.

"I don't know. I wasn't there. Does it help if you light candles?"

"Yes, because then everyone starts to pray and God listens and does what people ask. That's the mercy bit. If people ask for mercy, God gives mercy. Mercy is the same as being nice," Nora added, reflexively adding the definition.

"Nora, do you think my grandpa is happy?"

Nora gave her a face that reflected the ridiculousness of the question. "Of course he's happy, Andrea. He's with God. If you're with God, you're happy. That's the way it works."

"But don't you think he's a little bit sad? Don't you think he misses us?"

This was sticky. "Well, he might be a little bit sad." Nora used two fingers close together to show the smallest bit. "But he's a big, big bit happy." She spread her two arms wide apart. "He's having a ball. He's meeting all his dead friends. He's watching us talk right now, Andrea and he's thinking, poor Andrea. I wish she would be happy for me."

Andrea nodded, tears forming in her eyes. "I am happy for

him, Nora. Of course I am. I'll just miss him. I was a little worried about the swear words."

"Andrea, grown-ups have a hard time being good, too. They just don't get yelled at as much as we do. God knows about this. He understands. Grown-ups have to say they're sorry like everyone else. Then it's all over and into heaven they go."

"How do they get to heaven?"

"God comes and carries them."

Andrea thought about this. "My grandpa was big, Nora."

"God brings a couple of angels with Him and they help with the carrying if a person is heavy."

"What do the angels look like?"

Nora did not hesitate for a moment. "Like the tooth fairy. And they carry lots of money because people always pray for money. They're very strong. I wouldn't worry about your grandpa. They can manage big people."

Andrea let out a big, deep, healing sigh and smiled at her friend. "I feel better."

Nora smiled. "I'm happy for you, Andrea. You have a grandpa in heaven. Now we both do. My mom says they help us from heaven. So I figure we have someone helping us all the time, even when all of these guys are asleep. Andrea?"

"Yes?"

"Can we go tell my mom about your grandpa? She'll light the candles and we'll pray and ask God for the mercy. It's just to be sure," she hastened to add. "It's to be on the safe side."

"That would be good, Nora. I'd feel better if we did."

Nora took Andrea's hand in hers and solemnly brought her grieving friend in to her mother. Soon after, the candles were lit in front of the Sacred Heart of Jesus picture and Nora's family, in bathrobes and pajamas, asked Jesus to have mercy on Andrea's grandpa.

Part Three

Purgatory

Jesus

"There is an attempt to obscure the reality of the next life, life eternal. For this reason, many souls do not accept that they have an inheritance awaiting them. Poor souls. How discouraging for them to labor and suffer without understanding the purpose. Is it any wonder there is such an attempt to discover substitutes for true peace? My apostles understand that there is no value in being too comfortable in an earthly body because they will one day relinquish it. The body is not a god, for all the enemy would like to portray it as such. Each body is a creation of the Father. Each soul is a creation of the Father. Humanity, precious humanity, I want you to understand that you are cherished. I, Jesus, love you and cherish you. My enemy does not feel this way. My enemy seeks to hurt you. Do not reject Me. Spend time in silence, considering the remainder of your days on earth and how you would like to conduct yourself. The enemy cannot promise you that you will live forever. Only I can make that promise and only through Me will you find the Father, the One who loves you. Have no fear when considering the next life, regardless of your sins. If you repent, you will be saved. It is that simple. Repent and you will be saved. You will find a welcome in My Kingdom because My Kingdom is

your home. Be at peace, little soul. I am with you. I will take care of you."

May 18, 2006

"I wish to teach souls about My mercy. Souls should approach Me with the greatest confidence and joy. In order to assist souls in learning to trust Me and rely on My goodness, I have allowed this little glimpse into the process of purification. How joyful We are in heaven to welcome each soul to the Kingdom. I am Love and all souls in My Kingdom understand and practice divine love. There is no need to be protective or suspicious here. There is no barrier between each soul and My truth. There is no barrier between each soul and My acceptance. Be at peace, little souls of the world. Your God cherishes you and will care for you tenderly and mercifully when you arrive home from your time of exile. Proceed in joyful trust and you will be making the choice of the very wise ones. I give this information freely today because so many misjudge God or do not know God. I understand how this has happened, and yet I cannot allow it to continue. The children of God must know of My great mercy and compassion so that they can live in peaceful anticipation of their time in eternity. Along with this glimpse of purification, I am granting great graces of calm and trust. Dear little beloved soul, accept this gift from your Jesus and believe that you will be welcomed home when you arrive."

Purgatory

Today, Easter Sunday, was a happy and peaceful day. I went down to the chapel to pray. Jesus drew me into a state of union with Him and brought me to a place. It was further away from the place where it is a new day, over another sky and into another place of activity. He told me beforehand that He was taking me to show me where souls would go after they die. It was like a park, beautiful, peaceful. There were people there. I understood that some souls were newly arrived. They were with loved ones, talking and laughing. There was great lightness of spirit and initially I thought these were all children playing. They were not all children, though, although some were children. And they were not all family members in the earthly sense. They were members of our family of God.

In one area souls moved through the air. This was giving them great joy and they were laughing aloud. I understood that they were learning to move at will, to their delight. Jesus let me look for a while, and then drew me away to one end of the area that was misty. I walked into the mist and it became increasingly more and more misty and foggy. There were many souls in the mist. I could hear their prayers as I walked.

Jesus stopped me at one soul and I listened. This man sat up against a tree. He was completely isolated by the mist. He sat with his back to this tree praying. I could hear him. He pleaded with God, saying, "I'm sorry. I'm sorry." Grief for his sins poured out of him. He felt so much regret. Jesus said that this was a place where souls came to be purified. I understood that there were souls all around us. I also understood that as the mist thickened, so did the isolation and remorse.

I said, "Jesus, his prayers are so beautiful, so pure."

Jesus told me that all prayers in this place were beautiful and pure. The man was praying passionately that souls on earth, some of them his loved ones, would be spared such dreadful remorse. Jesus explained to me that this soul had worshipped a false god. He said that this man worshipped the god of materialism and rejected Him, Jesus. This man was being purified.

This was purgatory.

I understood that there were levels and that souls taken now are granted the most extreme mercy imaginable because of the darkness of this time. Jesus is making me write that. I resist it because then I have to listen to souls saying that this time is no darker than any other. This puts me in a position of proving what I cannot prove.

I have to say that I would be quite content to sit in the mist at that tree and tell God how much I loved Him and how sorry I was for my sins. You could pray for everyone on earth, you could praise God, you could do plenty of good there. If Jesus wants me there, I'll be happy to go.

I would hate to feel that sad about not serving Jesus, though. I assure any reader that this remorse is dreadful. Also, these souls did not see Jesus or experience Him as He went through there so they must be denied any awareness of God's presence, much as we are here on earth. In the most benign area, where I first entered, souls were with others, but they did not experience Christ. So the isolation lessened as souls became purified.

I was thinking about this experience later, of course, and something occurred to me. My first thought on arriving at this place was that it was a park for children. I understand that this impression came to me not because all of the souls were children, but because all of the souls were child-like in their joy and delight, much as I was that way when Jesus brought me to heaven. It must be that new arrivals are so awed and overjoyed that they become like children.

(I later understood that the souls in this area have just been freed from the mist of remorse.)

Jesus took me back with Him through the night skies, into the holy city where God the Father is, along with the saints. I understand that the souls in the city where it is a new day are united with Christ. They saw me when I was there. The souls in the holy city are obviously united with Christ. But the souls in purgatory did not seem to notice me or Jesus.

When I returned to myself I prayed for that man and begged Jesus to give him relief. I did not need to ask Jesus to forgive him as he is already forgiven or he would not have been in that place at all.

In purgatory the souls have a certainty that God exists. They know His goodness and they know the truth. Given this, they know that they will spend eternity with Him and with their loved ones. They are free of doubts.

Souls are benefiting the Kingdom with their prayers so they are useful. Surely that is a consolation to them.

April 22, 2006

Today our Lord brought me mystically to purgatory again. I went in through the park area. It was as beautiful as the last time. I was struck to silence by the beauty of the trees and the wind blowing through them. I could hear voices in the distance, much like one hears the voices of children playing at a distance on a summer night. Such peace and happiness. Jesus drew me in through the mist and today took me further back. It became darker and dimmer. It was grey, with heavier mist. Souls were even more isolated and turned into themselves, as it were.

I stopped at a woman praying. She was nearly curled up in a ball and rocking, so great was her distress at the damage she had done through her disobedience to Jesus on earth. Jesus revealed that she was a fortune teller and that she led many people astray. This woman was repeating over and over again, "I'm sorry. I'm sorry. I'm sorry." She was in terrific remorse, deservedly so, of course. That is a given. Everything here is just and fair. Jesus drew me away.

I could not leave her in this condition and said, "Jesus, please. What can I do?"

He was so kind and gentle. He said, ***"She will benefit from your intercession."***

At that very moment she stopped saying, "I'm sorry" and began saying, "Praise you, Jesus. Thank you, Jesus. Thank you for your goodness, Lord Jesus Christ."

I detected some measure of joy in that prayer now. Consoled, I followed Christ, aware of His mercy. They really need our intercession there. I am acutely aware that our cheerful obedience will do great things for them if we add a simple prayer here and there.

We moved into yet an even darker place. Souls here were so wrapped up in their misery that I could not even hear their prayers. They were not at a level where they were capable of prayer. I sought a word to describe what I felt here and the word I came up with was cheerless. These souls were destined for hell as they had worked actively against Christ and the Kingdom for the bulk of their lives. At the last moment, they chose Jesus and He brought them here. They are compelled, by justice and the need for cleansing and purification, to revisit each sin and each impact of each sin on the souls of others, as well as the impact on the souls impacted by others. This, surely, is a heavy but absolutely necessary burden. Again, these souls worked against God, often making war on His children.

I did not feel prompted to beg God for graces for these souls. I was reverent in the face of their total immersion into the evil of their lives. I was acutely aware of the mercy of our Jesus and the good and loving heart of our God. I thanked Him that these souls were saved and I know we will love them and enjoy them for all eternity. These souls are a triumph for us all. I loved them each so much. Praise God for each one of them and as I write this, I am asking God to move them along as quickly as possible.

Our Lord showed me a glimpse of one small area of hell at this time. I saw a soul with the ugliest red eyes. They are vacant, devoid of all humanity. They are evil.

This demon's eyes locked onto something and for a moment I thought it was me but he went right past me and began to assault another one such as himself. They are fighting constantly here. They are assaulting each other. They are molesting each other. They are shaming and humiliating each other. They are in the right place. I felt no fear as they cannot hurt us and I know it.

I shifted my gaze and saw the most ominously evil being. It sat in a place by itself, immersed in darkness of thought. I said, "Jesus, what is he doing?" Jesus explained that he was plotting against the Church. I felt a momentary fear for Pope Benedict. Jesus said that he could not hurt Pope Benedict because of the Holy Father's obedience. He explained and I "saw" clearly that if a soul is obedient to the Church, that soul seals off gaps where the enemy can enter and work. This wretch could plot against the Pope until the cows come home but our beloved leader will always be safe through his obedience.

Other poor souls will allow this demon influence through their pride and subsequent disobedience, but those who stand firm under the protection of Church authority will be safe. I was amazed at how impenetrable a soul can become this way, through obedience.

Suddenly, like a snake striking, this demon lashed out and grabbed another soul, pulling him into his dungeon-like area to torture him. This victim, far from being a sympathetic figure, would be tortured for a while and then move off to plot against and victimize another.

Again, I did not feel sympathy for any of these. I felt that Christ was smart to contain these ones where they could make war on each other and leave God's children alone. God's children are vulnerable through sin and persistence in sin but where there is any remorse or humility or even a little bit of love, God protects. I must say, I was repelled, disgusted, even a little upset, but not afraid and not startled. I have seen souls behaving in similar manners in life.

April 23, 2006

Jesus brought me again to purgatory. I found that I was back in the park area. I rested by a large tree that I had seen the last time. Jesus indicated a bridge, which I studied. The reason I was interested in the construction of the bridge is because it was so artistically built with beautiful stone, sanded down to smoothness, and stones all intricately arranged. It crossed over a stream, arching a bit in the middle. I considered that souls had designed this in heaven and built it here and I thought it was a beautiful example that Christ will use any talents we might have.

Jesus prompted me to cross over and I did. I found myself in an area where people sat together at round tables and talked. I moved between the tables and listened. People were from different time periods, but they were all at this same area of purification. I heard statements like the following:

I did not accept God's grace.

I refused to open myself to His help.

I see that I did not want God's help.

I prevented God from enlightening me.

It was clear to me that these souls were helping each other to understand where they rejected Christ in their lives on earth. This park-like area is the final area of purgatory. These souls were all still in purgatory, still completing their purification process.

It was always clear to me that the best way to help someone with an alcohol addiction was to refer them to Alcoholics Anonymous. That program of 12 steps relies on God's grace to move souls through a process of accepting mistakes and taking responsibility. Additionally, I have seen that a support group for victims, made up of victims, is most beneficial in helping souls to come to terms with being abused.

This seemed similar in that souls were voluntarily examining where they had rejected God in their lives, thereby rejecting His grace so that they would not have to change. Souls were helping each other to understand where and how they had taken turns against Christ. These souls had long since been confronted with their sins and made reparation for them. This, the end of the purification process, was a more gentle, higher level of self-acceptance and awareness. A big part of the healing came from the acceptance and understanding of their brothers and sisters around them, who were involved in the same part of the process.

I asked Jesus how our prayers affected these souls, given

what I understand that they cannot help themselves. He said that our prayers help a soul to move through the process more quickly.

I asked about the souls who had nobody to pray for them. He said that many prayers are offered for souls who are already in heaven. These prayers are applied with perfect justice to others. The concept of perfect justice, by the way, is one that I could rest in for two weeks if I had the time because it takes into account all that has ever happened as well as all that will ever happen. It is way too advanced for my brain but it would be fun to sit with, all the same. What struck me most in this area was the love that these souls had for each other. There was such camaraderie and understanding and acceptance. I noted different races, by the way, as well as different periods, which told me that souls take different amounts of time to get through purgatory because some souls were from a more modern era than others. All were at peace and all were content and contemplative in their self-examination.

Another feature that jumped out at me was the total absence of falseness. There is no phoniness, no fake humility or pretending to care about someone. It's all perfectly honest and perfectly safe, emotionally speaking, as well as every other way of speaking.

Jesus prompted me to cross over yet another bridge, not exactly the same as the last but also beautifully designed and built. I did, after admiring the bridge itself, and found myself in another area. This was the same park, but an area separated from the last and actually the last stop in purgatory before going to heaven.

This is what I saw. Souls were with others, not all of whom were from purgatory. Jesus allowed me to know that souls in this area could see and talk to souls who could come to them from heaven. In other words, souls in heaven can visit loved ones here in this last area. I understood that they come to bring them to Christ. This is distinct from other areas of purgatory, where souls from heaven can check in on loved ones but the loved one in purgatory cannot see or interact with them, in the same way that we on earth do not have the eyes to see these heavenly souls when they are near us.

My understanding is this and I know that someone will correct me if I am getting this wrong. Souls in heaven can visit souls in purgatory but the soul in purgatory cannot see them or hear them without exceptional grace. This is the very same as with us here on earth. We know God exists, despite our doubts. We know God speaks to us, despite our inability to hear Him with our ears.

As my six-year-old son said, "God is invisible and we cannot see Him. His words must be invisible too because I can't hear them."

There are no separations in heaven. There is freedom. So if I am in purgatory and my sister is in heaven, she can come to me and see how I am getting on. She can pray for me, intercede for me, and bring me comfort. I will not necessarily know that it is she who obtains graces for me, but I will feel the progress in my growth and be consoled.

In this area, the last area before heaven, souls are coming to a final acceptance of their mistakes. This acceptance will last them for eternity. There is no judging of each other in this land of God, which includes purgatory and heaven. Souls are far too busy coming to terms with their own mistakes to point fingers at anyone else. I love it here. I love the honesty, directness, calmness, beauty, and certainty of God and His goodness. There is complete safety from ridicule or attack. I assure my reader that this purgatory is part of the heavenly

Kingdom and not a bad place to be. Compared to earth, it is wonderful, regardless of the area you land in.

Back to the final area, Jesus said, *"Anne, this is the most grace-filled area of purgatory. Let Me show you the grace."*

With that, I sensed Him lift His arm and suddenly I saw the most beautiful blue sparkling rays of light. This light came from above and flowed slowly and continuously down into this area. I saw some souls talking together, in particular a woman talking to a man. She was a saint, already a heavenly resident, and she was here to bring this man to heaven. I thought they were brother and sister, but I do not know for certain. They loved each other and had known each other on earth. He was timid and she took him by the hand and gently urged him. There was such joy. Finally, he allowed himself to be pulled up into the blue light and away they went to heaven.

I said, "Lord, souls are a little timid. What if nobody is praying for them? Do they get stuck here, like in immigration?"

Jesus laughed. He said, *"No. Every so often Our mother, Mary, will come and take everyone who is here, in this area. Here is another way it happens."*

I saw a man sitting perfectly still. I knew he was ready to go to Jesus, but he was also timid. I looked up, into the light, and the man did also. I had an awareness of Christ being up in the light. I sensed Jesus smiling at this man and extending His hand. The man gave a cry of joy and rose immediately to Christ with his arms out. From my vantage point I saw Jesus wrap His arms around this man and move off into the light with him.

"That is another way it happens, Anne."

Nobody is left to languish when they are ready, it seems. I

did not do justice to the ethereal quality of the light, which is actually special grace.

Jesus took me away into the misty area again. In it, He stopped me at a young boy. The boy was praying for his father, earnestly and with great passion. (I was going to say with great worry but that is the wrong word. Clearly, though, this boy wanted his father helped in a compelling way.)

Jesus listened to his prayers. I understood that there had been an accident and the father had been at fault. This boy died as a result of the accident and the father was walking down a path of sin in his anguish. The boy, who had no ill feelings for his father, only love, begged for graces.

"Your father will be assisted, My son," Jesus said to the boy's soul, without words. The boy's prayers calmed and quieted and suddenly the mist around him lightened and he could hear the voices of those in the park area, as I related before, much like on a summer evening, where you hear children playing in the distance. The reason this is significant is because it is the first indication of the total isolation lifting. The soul had advanced to a lighter area of purgatory in our Lord's mercy.

I understood that this soul was not a boy, but rather a young man of 22 when he died on earth. The prayers are so pure and beautiful that they seem to come from children who are innocent and honest and loving.

We moved on, back into the deepest part of purgatory. I asked Jesus the difference between this darkest area of purgatory and hell. Jesus said that the two places were separated by eternity but that the choice between hell and purgatory is often a hair's breath of a difference. I understood that our prayers, our offering of our day to Jesus, and then our little teeny sacrifices accepted for Christ, as well as our greatest pain and sufferings offered for Christ, can actually help make the difference between a soul choosing Christ or casting himself away from Him into hell. I cannot think of anyone I know who belongs in hell.

Souls in this cheerless, dark place are wrapped into themselves. They are studying each of their actions and the impact their actions had on everyone affected. It's not a pretty thing to have to do if you have spent your life rejecting Christ and indeed working against Him. Most souls were silent and still. One whimpered and shifted in anguish.

I said, "Lord, what can we do for them? How can we help them?"

Jesus said, *"Look."*

I saw Our Lady walking through the darkness putting her little hand on each soul. I heard her whispering, *"Shh. God loves you. Be at peace. You are loved."* The whimpering soul quieted after she touched him. How our poor little mother loves us. We must all help her as much as possible because it is this suffering she seeks to prevent.

One thing I have to remark upon is this. Souls are safe here. They are protected. Nobody can hurt anyone else. This area, after all, is God's area and God has custody of each soul. God has all the power. This is His jurisdiction and all is orderly. God would never allow a soul to be injured in His care and these souls, while they are in their own private "hell" if you will, with remorse, are safe and protected. What a contrast to the real hell, where souls constantly prey upon each other.

April 25, 2006

Today the Lord asked me to go with Him to see a soul in purgatory. We crossed the Holy City and stopped for a time so that our Lord could instruct me on some details of the mission. We then crossed the deep night sky, over the busy new day land, and then out into another night sky, not as deep as the first. We ended up in the park area, where I rested in the beauty. Jesus drew me into the mist, stopping at a woman. She prayed with great fervor and passion, asking God to prevent other souls from making a mistake that she had made when she was young. I understood the mistake to be an abortion. As we stood nearby, listening to her beautiful prayers, the mist around her began to lighten. Mist blew past her in patches that became lighter and lighter. Eventually, after a short time, she found herself kneeling in the sunshine of the park perimeter. Jesus said, *"Rise."*

She had the most dignified look of calm peace on her face as she rose and walked into the new area. She looked around as though she had always known that this was her destination, and then walked off to join a group of people standing near a stream and bridge. As she approached the group, a man stood back and extended his hand to her. His smile was filled with happiness and welcome. This woman joined them effortlessly as though they were from the closest, most loving family on earth. She was on her way into the last process.

Jesus told me many things. The previous day had been extremely difficult. My trust is down to nearly zero and I can't seem to reclaim it. Anyway, I spent the day making acts of love and obedience to Jesus.

He said, *"What you saw was the direct result of one of your simple acts of obedience during your difficult day. Anne, did you see the difference? This treasured soul moved with the greatest speed through her purification. She was cleansed and healed and edified. You, Anne, will be credited for the merciful speed with which she progressed. Do you see My generosity? Proclaim that generosity so that souls will live their lives in union with Me. I will reward every soul so bountifully for their allegiance, Anne. I will reward their loved ones. The fruits of their commitment to the cause of the Savior will astound them. Anne, these times are dark for humanity. This woman would never have chosen to reject her child in another time. You saw her goodness. You saw her love for Me. She, like many others, suffered from the grave deception of the enemy. I protected her in the end, of course, and she will give glory and joy to others for all eternity. There will be a joyous reunion for her and her child. But such pain she experienced!"*

Jesus pauses at this and I feel that His pain is from her grief and the grief of every woman like her who suffers anguish resulting from an abortion. Jesus is hurting because they are hurting, just as we apostles often hurt because He is hurting. Poor, poor Jesus. How much He loves us.

"Anne, be at peace in My plan. It is My plan after all. I will send you the trust you require and with it you must communicate trust to others. Move slowly, remaining in the present, content to represent Me when you are asked to do so. It is all My work. It is all My effort that is required. Peace and calm are the right of each apostle."

April 26, 2006

Today the Lord drew me into His heart and brought me back to the park area in purgatory. I rested there and He began to speak. He explained the following.

When we celebrate a funeral on earth, they also celebrate it in heaven. Many of the soul's relations will attend, going back many generations. There will be many angels there, who had anything at all to do with that soul's life. Additionally, souls in purgatory who knew the soul will be aware of that soul's death and pray. Great graces are made available for that soul's initial progress in the process of purgation. I asked our Lord if the soul himself is present. Jesus said the soul has already placed himself in the exactly appropriate location in the process so the soul in purgatory is aware of the great graces and prayers and sacrifices because that soul is feeling the benefit of them.

The answer is "yes" in that there are no separations in the heavenly Kingdom but the soul is not present in the way a soul in heaven could be present. The soul in purgatory does not have the same awareness that the soul in heaven enjoys. I thought of all of the Masses said for some souls and Jesus said that these all help a soul and if the soul has no need of them, they are passed to another so nothing is wasted. Jesus also said that if a soul lived a life aimed at Christ, that soul can complete the purgative process by the end of the funeral. It is really important that when we go to a funeral, we actually pray for the deceased. If we find ourselves deep in thought over the fact that our shoes do not match our purses, we will know we are doing it wrong.

My understanding, based on today's conversation, is this. A person dies. That soul sees the truth in God's presence. God's light is so revealing, so complete and perfect, that there is no question of if or maybe. It is and that's it. In other words, there won't be a lot of dialogue about why a soul did this or that. It will be there in front of the soul with all mitigation and aggravation factored in for him.

Let's examine a sin according to a criminal code. You

might commit a Class 2 felony, severe enough, but when you meet Christ it might become a Class 4 felony, less severe, given the circumstances under which you made the decision.

In the same way, a sin that may be considered mild may elevate to a more severe level given the aggravating circumstances that surround it, as in level of malice and intent to cause harm.

Sins confessed and answered for will not be held against a soul but the soul will have to come to terms with those experiences in order to be at peace. Christ will forgive but the soul may have a little acceptance work to do.

One thing is for certain. This is the Land of Perfect Truth and any nonsense will dissipate immediately upon entry. Falseness is not even an option or a possibility here. It cannot be. All is truth.

We are discussing this as in the context of an awareness of sin. This is fine because it is accurate, but what is more important is the joy that surrounds a soul who dies and enters into the truth of eternity. Who can describe the happiness a soul experiences who finds that God and heaven are far beyond their expectations or any hope they harbored? In addition, there is the fact that when a soul dies he enters into God's love with perfect awareness. These souls in purgatory are not distressed. They are prayerful and humble, childlike in their knowledge that they are loved and cherished and important to God. These souls understand that the work they are doing in purgatory, they are doing with God for the peace and benefit of their souls. It is all so good and perfect that words fail me and I wonder at God entrusting this heavenly Kingdom to the words that come from me.

I think a good thing for me to say here is that it is an impossible thing for a soul to be disappointed in God's mercy, in God's love, or in God's commitment to total healing for every soul. Our reward for even the smallest act of kindness or allegiance will be magnificent. Our joy in the fellowship and love of our brothers and sisters will be immeasurable. These are wonderful people there. And they love us. Every soul can be assured that he or she will be welcomed and loved.

April 28th, 2006

Today our Lord brought me back to purgatory. I rested there and He began to show me what occurred on Christmas Day. I felt great joy and happiness and began to see souls around in the park. As I watched the perimeter, where the mists begin, I could see the mist moving back, lightening, and the boundary of fog actually dissipating. Souls began to walk from the mist. I saw two people join hands happily and walk into the park area laughing and smiling. Everyone seemed expectant. It was a beautiful time there.

I sensed Our Lady's presence and it made my heart ache with loneliness for her. She was definitely a big part of the joy. Jesus said that souls in heaven participate in Christmas with great giving. Graces and joys are exchanged and granted and many souls are shown special mercy and brought to heaven from purgatory. Jesus said that on Christmas Day, all souls advance in purgatory, regardless of their location or level. Jesus said that all souls on earth are granted graces on Christmas and that all souls in heaven experience graces on Christmas. He said it is an important day because it celebrates God's great love for humanity by His willingness to become one of us by being born into the world through Mary. This makes all of these souls happy.

I can't describe it completely but it has something to do with each soul experiencing personally the profound and unique love that God has for that soul. It's almost as though Christ were born specifically and totally for every one of us and on Christmas Day each soul gets an enhanced awareness of the gift that His humanity was and is for us individually. This was a joyous day and it made me aware again that the heavenly Kingdom is vibrant with activity and action.

April 30th, 2006

Today our Lord brought me over the heavenly Kingdom. He stopped in the Valley of Solitude and I looked down at the stream, forest, mountains and valleys. Jesus said, *"This is all for you, Anne. Do you understand?"*

Indeed I did. At that moment, I understood the smallest bit of truth that all that is in heaven belongs very personally to each one of us in a separate and complete way. It is similar to the understanding I had that Jesus walked the earth each day for each one of us separately. Each Bible story has something to say to each of us on any given day and Jesus actually lived each day thinking of each one of us, almost as though He had lived a separate and complete life for every one of us.

Perhaps this truth is self-evident to others. I never understood it until today and I know that I got only the barest glimpse of understanding. When Jesus said, *"This is all for you, Anne,"* He spoke the truth.

That truth is just as true for every single one of us.

We went over the Holy City and over the night sky, over the new day city and out again into the lighter night sky, and on again into the park. Jesus began to talk about souls. He said that purgatory prompts and completes the process of self-acceptance. Jesus explained this.

Some souls understand that Jesus exists. They believe in God. They do not live this belief, however, and they do not make decisions based on their belief. They do not serve.

Some souls understand that Jesus exists. They believe in God. They make many decisions based on this belief and live good lives. They serve partially.

Some souls understand that Jesus exists. They believe in God. They live this belief and make most or all of their decisions based on this belief. These souls are saints. They serve in near totality.

It is a challenge for a person to conform his life to something he has not seen but therein lay the merit of our earthly service. We do not see this heavenly Kingdom. We do not see the saints who have gone before us. We cannot touch the stones or trees or water in heaven. We are, however, given great grace in our souls with which to understand and believe the truths of God. The Sacraments provide treasures of grace to strengthen our understanding of God.

Souls who live for the world deny these truths. They do not wish to believe because they do not wish to serve God. They desire their own will. When these souls die, they have to come to terms with the fact that they knew God existed and chose against Him on some occasions. They have to admit and acknowledge that they knew of God's existence because this is the land of truth and there is no bantering or word play. The truth is plain to see here.

On earth souls try to tie each other up in knots with clever arguments designed to distract from the truth. This will not work in the heavenly Kingdom. We will be able to relax there and there will be no need to be clever in that respect. This will be a relief because one gets tired of having to constantly expose the enemy's distortions and traps. I find that some souls try to put me in a paper bag with their words and I am always trying to fight my way out. I am at peace about this, as every soul should be. When we are being challenged and we lack the words, we must simply say nothing. Ultimately, it is God's fight, not ours. He always wins in the end. The worst scenario is that Jesus will find me an inadequate servant. Well, that's just fine by me. Jesus already knows I am inadequate.

With regard to the three distinctions in the way a soul responds to the knowledge of God, each soul will have to come to terms with his response to the grace that was given to him on earth. This is what purgatory does for us. It aligns our life on earth, our service and non-service, to the reality that is heaven. We see heaven before us. Behind us is our response to the grace given to us on earth, otherwise known as the truth of our life. We must make the journey from one to the other. The two have to be merged in order for us to be ready for eternity.

It's good, I find. This process is a good thing. It is another aspect of God's great and perfect mercy.

Jesus brought me to a woman praying in the mists. She prayed heartbreakingly for her husband. I understood that she had blocked God's grace in their family. Her husband, destined for a high level of holiness, had not been allowed to bring his faith into their home and family. This woman had ridiculed him and mocked him until he remained silent about his feelings for God.

Her remorse was pitiful. She begged God selflessly not to allow her husband to be held accountable. She was asking that she be allowed to take responsibility for his not achieving the level of holiness he should have achieved.

Jesus answered her prayer and told me that in the last days of his life, her husband would advance in holiness at a miraculous pace, allowing him to be as holy as he would have become given a sympathetic and accepting atmosphere in the home. I gather he did not fight for his faith with his wife and it is for this she fears he will be held accountable.

I see that this man chose to keep the peace in his family with good motives of family unity. God is rewarding this and granting exceptionally gracious graces in response to the prayers of this wife and mother because their children will be affected profoundly by their father's holiness in this, his last agony on earth.

I was glad to know this but I could not bear that this woman be left here in the mists. I begged Jesus for something for her and the mists began moving gently, blowing away. She rose to walk into the final area but first stopped and smiled in our direction. It was a beautiful smile, filled with gratitude to God.

I said, "Lord, does she know we are here?"

He said, *"Yes, but she does not see us."*

Jesus

May 5, 2006

"Anne, you suffer from the falseness of others. Understand that this is temporary. You know that in the heavenly Kingdom, all is truth. Be at peace in the temporary suffering that I will for you as I will not allow My mission to be damaged to the degree that its effectiveness is lessened. If you walk with Me, you walk with truth. All around you may be lies and falseness, but in

your soul there is My heavenly truth and the knowledge that all souls in heaven rest in truth. Souls on earth may be fooled by falseness, but they will have perfect knowledge when they arrive here. The lies of the enemy cannot hurt you any more than I allow. Let this comfort you and give you courage. If it is My will that a soul suffer in this way, then I must be allowed freedom to work in the soul of the victim. I want only what is best for humanity. To that end I allow a certain amount of suffering for My friends. Be at peace because no soul that follows Me will be abandoned to the enemy of truth. You will find that the greater the suffering on earth, the greater the glory for heaven."

May 7, 2006

On this day our Lord showed me that souls who follow Him on earth can come directly to heaven. I understood that souls who come right to heaven spend some time enjoying and becoming accustomed to unity with Jesus in a place like the Valley of Solitude. I love it there because I love the forest. I understood though that some souls will find themselves near an ocean or a desert or another kind of place. The place where they become accustomed to unity with Jesus will be totally pleasing to each individual. This is only the beginning of heaven for each of us.

Because there are no separations in heaven, a soul is not confined to this area and is free to move at will. That stated, the soul will be in such a state of bliss and wonder that the soul will require some time to remain with the Lord and become comfortable with His continual and blessed presence.

Jesus said that most souls should come more or less directly to heaven. God is not unreasonable and He did not make it too difficult to live a holy life on earth. It is simple really. I understood that in this time fewer souls go directly to heaven than in other times because fewer souls are living in holy simplicity according to God's will. God is not pleased with this, of course.

When Jesus showed me the mist of purgatory again I understood something. I understood that the mist is not punishment, but rather a mercy, because the mist in purgatory insures privacy. Souls would not like their sins to be exposed for others to see, and the work that needs to be done in the misty part of purgatory is a private thing. For Jesus to allow souls to complete this work in the mist is another act of mercy for souls.

I understand that it is said that all will be exposed. This is true. But it is not a 'stand around in a circle and condemn the sinner' kind of exposure, from what I can see. It is a compelling light of understanding that lays bare our individual souls and motives. I assure each reader that everyone will be too concerned with their own flaws to spend any time pointing at the flaws of another.

This is so important that I want to do it justice. God allows us the grace of examining our soul in privacy so that our grief and remorse will be visible only to Him and to the saints who wish to help us. The work done in our souls is very deeply personal. As I understand it, purgatory is a process of forgiving ourselves and coming to terms with our decisions against our good God. Depending on the sins and the level of malice, it takes more or less time.

For example, if I punch my sister in the face when I am six years old, I have to repent and consider the impact of the mistake on my sister. This takes a little time and most children apologize and become peaceful in a short time. But the apology and the realization that the act was wrong is crucial if the child is to proceed in goodness and self-acceptance.

If I take a gun and shoot my sister in the head when I am thirty, how much more will I have to repent and consider the impact of the mistake on my sister and on the world? The act is more serious, more impacting on both the world and the Kingdom of God, and on my sister. I will need to take a great deal of time, I would think, coming to terms with my mistake and proceeding in self-acceptance.

Souls should understand that the important work is done in the soul or heart of the sinner. Getting caught doing something wrong can be good in that it can force one to come to terms with a mistake. Being held accountable can prompt the sinner to do the work in the soul. This work, this coming to terms with our own failures, is done in silence, in contemplation.

I am struck powerfully again with the fact that we will have to do the work before or after death. Nobody will enter heaven without a good long think on their behaviors and actions. This deepens my understanding of the Lord's constant urging that souls spend time in silence. If we are always distracted by noise and entertainment we will not be inclined or able to scrutinize ourselves. This self scrutiny must be done.

I thought immediately of souls in cloisters or monasteries where a good deal of time is spent in silence and prayer. These souls have an excellent chance of going right to heaven, I would think, because they are willingly remaining in silence, which encourages self scrutiny and heavenly light. They are submitting to silence and time with Christ before their death.

I also thought of prisoners. Prison would be an excellent place to become a saint. I would tell all prisoners that if they walk with Christ and examine their consciences in silence, they will be much further along than most souls not in prison.

I asked Jesus about all of our past sins. I know many souls who grieve deeply about the sins in their past. Jesus said that these souls will not suffer from their past sins if they confess them and are sorry for them. Grief over sins is an indication that a soul is doing the work here on earth, which will free the soul from doing the work after death.

Penance, in the spirit of holding one's self accountable, is not a bad thing. By this I refer to little sacrifices in the day, small fasts, completing an action for another, and generally offering extra service or love in the spirit of reparation. Holy souls often offer sacrifices and penances in reparation for the sins of others, which is good also.

I pictured souls climbing the mountain of holiness and imagined holy souls. Holy souls enter the mist on earth by denying themselves and taking up their crosses. On any given day a soul climbs the mountain of holiness with a cross strapped to his back. When I pictured this I saw souls climbing with cross-shaped backpacks. Some were very heavy, I could see. As a soul gets holier, that burden, that cross becomes less penitential in terms of necessity and more to do with the salvation of others.

A holy soul moving toward Christ on the mountain who is suffering from cancer, for example, could have thousands of souls strapped to his tired back. The need for penance, perhaps, has passed as possibly this soul has aligned his will to Christ's and made amends for any sins committed before his soul was aligned with heaven's will. Any of the more minor sins committed while the soul was serving God are also being answered for as the soul climbs. At this time, the act of carrying a cross in union with Christ obtains great benefits for many souls in need of conversion. Perhaps, and this is usually quite true, this soul is marching up the mountain because of the sacrifice of another who has gone before him. He owes the Kingdom, yes, and he not only repays, but gives God much more than he owes so that others may benefit. This type of soul will not require time in purgatory because he has willingly walked in the mist of silence and suffering on earth.

If a soul is marching up the mountain of holiness and the soul is suffering, that soul is allowed to become tired and discouraged. Again, God is not unreasonable and our humanity delights Him. Another marching soul might enter the soul's little climbing area on the mountain and throw down her cross for a moment, sitting alongside this soul. The two can sit in silence, enjoying the companionship, or they can compare the struggles, encouraging and affirming one another. This fellowship is beautiful. This is an advance glimpse of the latter area of purgatory because souls help each other to come to terms with mistakes and struggles in God's light.

It is good to offer up our suffering, but remember that it is acceptable to rely on the support of other souls. In helping us, others can advance themselves.

In applying this to life, I see that the act of removing an errant child from the company of the family is a good thing. It may feel like a punishment to the child, but in reality it is merciful to give the child the opportunity to consider his behavior and amend his countenance in privacy. To let a child behave badly and remain in the companionship of others is counterproductive as the child has no opportunity to think it all over. This certainly will assure many parents who choose time-outs for discipline. Also worthy of consideration is the need to turn off the televisions for at least some period of time each day or week. We must reduce the noise in our lives. The constant din is seriously affecting our souls.

May 14, 2006

I saw a very large Consecrated Host elevated high up on a pedestal that was stone. It was the biggest, most solid pillar I have ever seen. There were people all around it, throngs, millions of souls. I saw some gazing up at Jesus in the Eucharist and they were enrapt with His purity and goodness and love. I saw a Sister and a priest whom I recognized and both looked steadily at Christ on this pedestal. They faced Him.

I saw others standing up close to the pedestal. Some were religious and some were lay. Some did not look up at Christ, but looked out at the throngs of people and drew attention to themselves and their proximity to the pedestal or the base that holds Christ. When souls approached the ones who were facing Christ, they also turned their gaze upward and began to adore Him. When souls approached the ones at the base who were not gazing up at Christ but out into the world, they sometimes turned and found the Eucharist on the pedestal and moved away from the ones who wanted to divert attention from Christ on to themselves.

Other times, people encountering those who drew attention to themselves became angry and bitter, disillusioned and wounded because of the falseness of the ones who stood by Christ claiming a holiness they did not possess or desire. The disappointed ones sometimes wandered back into the throngs, away from Christ and holy souls. These souls were repelled by the ugliness of falseness. They sometimes began to work against Christ, using as justification the ones who stood close to the pedestal but did not give glory to God. This was painful to see and those souls who behave falsely will have to answer for some of the damage done by the ones who are led astray by their falseness.

I asked Jesus what we should do about this situation, when we encounter souls such as this. It is extremely difficult as it is clear that they use their proximity to the Eucharist, to God, to advance their personal causes, be those causes financial, psychological, efforts to obtain control or superiority over others, or power.

Jesus said, *"Lead by example. Do not become distracted. Keep your eyes fixed on Me at all times and you will not be as personally disturbed."*

As upsetting as it is to view situations such as this, we must understand that it is far more upsetting to Christ because He is losing souls over this. I understand that it has always been this way and that helps a little. I am thinking of the Pharisees who pretended to be holy but had no love.

Jesus mitigates in every possible way, of course, and uses the proximity of the soul to draw people to Him. By this I mean that a soul seeking Christ will find Him because Christ will not hide. Souls drawn to a false one because of their apparent proximity to God will look upward and find God. They will gradually move deeper into the divine and away from the false one. There is no denying the fact, however, that souls wounded by this falseness sometimes do not recover. Sometimes they reject God.

I assure each reader that every consideration is made for one who is tricked or victimized by falseness. And it is true that God flows great good through these souls because as we have said, a soul seeking Christ will never be disappointed in his search. There will be perfect justice. Souls injured by those who claim to serve God and do not, are compensated.

God will never be unjust. It is not even possible for God to be unjust.

We must all remember to keep our eyes on Christ at all times.

Jesus drew me away, into the park in purgatory. He told me that He wanted to bring me to a soul. We travelled into the mist and I saw a man praying. He was a priest. This man was filled with remorse because when he served on earth, he did not pay the proper respect to Jesus in the Eucharist. He believed in the true presence, but did not pay homage to this presence. He set an example of casual indifference and even disrespect to God this way. I understood that this poor man ridiculed others who did respect God's presence in the Eucharist. This was causing him the greatest pain now and He prayed passionately. He was not exactly praying for forgiveness.

Jesus asked me twice to listen to him because I was not paying attention to what he was saying but to his deep remorse. This priest was begging Jesus to allow him to take responsibility for the sins of others who were led astray by his mistreatment of the Eucharist. He felt responsible. I asked Jesus if this were accurate, that he was responsible.

Jesus said it was not entirely accurate because many of the souls affected should have known better. For those who did not know better, the sin is less. This man wants to accept some responsibility. He does not wish to leave purgatory until all those he negatively impacted have moved through. Jesus will decide if this is just but I got the feeling that God is about to put this lovely man into heaven. Jesus has mitigated the damage to others, partially through this man's prayers. Some of the responsibility comes from the omission of graces that could and should have been obtained by this priest had he kept his eyes on Christ in loving obedience.

I wondered if people ever served their pugatory time in the place where they committed sin. Jesus explained this all very beautifully. He said that since there are no separations, heaven and earth are joined, but we lack the heavenly eyes to see that souls can be anywhere. Here is the distinction He made. If a soul is in purgatory, he is still in divine care or custody, if you will. Only God can decide where that soul can be. Because there is no denial allowable in heaven or in the heavenly Kingdom, it is possible that God will decide that a soul revisit the scene of his sin so that he can rest in it in order to absorb it fully because the soul must take responsibility for his sin. This may be the only way the soul can heal and come to full unity with God. In a situation where a soul struggles with this, God will place him there for a period.

Of course I asked about the devil's slaves. He said, yes, they can also be in places as well. I said, "Lord, can these holy souls in the purification process assist souls on earth in the places they might be resting in their sin?" He said, *"Of course. They pray for the souls who might be struggling."* For example, the priest I saw could have spent time in the churches where he so badly offended God. While he is there, you can bet that if there is another priest struggling with a similar temptation, this priest would have beseeched heaven to help the struggling one to avoid the same sins. This is how they love in purgatory and heaven. Everyone is pulling for everyone else. God allows this. It is all part of the family model that is the Communion of Saints.

Jesus drew my attention to souls I have seen from the next world. Souls in purgatory are always with Him, in that I sense that He has brought them to me. The saints are different when they come because they are permanently and forever united to the divine will. They have autonomy in some way. They come, as opposed to being brought. The souls He has allowed to communicate with me from purgatory are brought and are then taken back. That's how I understand it and I submit completely to the Church in this and everything.

May 15, 2006

Today our Lord helped me to understand many things about this mission. Afterwards, He brought me to an area in the park of purgatory. I had never been to this little corner and Jesus encouraged me to open my eyes and look around. There is a great tendency to be lazy and simply rest with Jesus, but that is not why the Lord is allowing this for me so I have to do as I am told.

I found myself in a most beautiful flower garden. I could sense the creativity of the gardener and I understood that this garden was designed in heaven by one of our brothers or sisters gone before us. It had the feel of spontaneity, but also a lovely order about the heights and colors. Clearly, this was a manifestation of how one gardener envisioned perfect order in a flower garden and I thought of my sister and how she would love to be given such a joyful project. I must add that I could also understand the great love and tenderness that the gardener had for the souls who were at this place in their process of purification. Everyone loves each other in this Kingdom of God and there is only tenderness and understanding for each other.

Jesus directed my attention down and away from this little corner and asked me what I saw. Initially, I thought it was the ocean but on closer inspection I saw a big lake. I could see across, far, to the other side where there were trees and a mountain but this was quite far away. The waves coming in were steady and gentle, lapping against the sandy shore. The ocean can be furious and pounding. In contrast, this little lake was not threatening, but beckoning.

Jesus compelled me to look closer, out into the lake. I did so and saw small boats. He drew my attention to one in particular and after that moment it was the only one I saw. In this boat lay a man. He looked young but I later understood that he had died as an old man who lived to what we would consider a great age. Everyone looks a lot better here and he struck me as fit and strong. He was lying on his back in this little boat with his back and shoulders and head propped up comfortably. His hands were behind his head and he was gazing up to the sky. I looked up to see what he was looking at and the sky became a deep silent night sky. The depth perception of this night sky was remarkable and this man could not take his eyes off the study of God's universe in all of the stars and planets. I don't know anything about stars and planets but I could not take my eyes off it either.

I asked Jesus what work this man was doing as I understood that he was growing and learning and advancing. Jesus said he was preparing for unity with God. He was in the final stage of learning about the Creator and the Creator's mastery over all. This man, who had an innocent boyish quality about him, was absorbing the omnipotence of God, along with the perfect benevolence of God. In some way, God the Father was gazing right back at him and the man was basking in God's love. It was a very personal moment between this man and his God and I revelled again in the uniqueness of each of our relationships with our Father. Imagine the greatest innocent wonder you have ever encountered and you will grasp the smallest joy of this scene.

In this soul, the longing for God grew and grew. He was getting to a place where his soul would naturally melt into heaven and unity with God. God drew him like the most powerful magnet draws a safety pin and I could feel his longing.

I must tell the reader that I wanted to jump in the water and swim out to this boat and climb in with him, so that I, too, could enjoy this experience. But that would never be right because one could not pierce his adoration of his God. Also, it reminded me of the pedestal. I saw the way this man looked up at his God and I was compelled to look also.

But isn't this the way we are asked to proceed? Isn't this what God keeps trying to tell us? Jesus says, ***"If you climb your mountain of holiness, others will follow."*** We have to keep our eyes on Christ and He will draw us up the mountain. Other souls will fall in behind us and alongside us and we will move, one after the other, away from danger and into the Father's Kingdom. Any soul who witnessed this scene of peace and contentment would give anything to be in this man's place. And this is only purgatory!

Something that bears mention is the normality of the scene. I listened carefully and I could hear the occasional small wave slapping against the boat. The boat rocked with the rise and fall of the water. The man seemed to shift on occasion. I could hear the waves coming into the shore. I could feel a breeze. This was mystical, I know, or I could not have been there, but it was also very real and concrete. I am at a loss to understand how God gets this done but I suppose it is like I am putting on borrowed glasses and with them I can see, hear, and feel these things. When Jesus takes the glasses back, I am here with a list of household chores to complete but I will not forget the beauty of this scene.

May 15, 2006

Jesus brought me to Him and allowed me to ask Him
questions about my personal spirituality. I get discouraged,
as I am not as good as I should be and often fail in charity
and patience. Jesus said that great holiness is something that
is achieved by practice and if we are willing to practice, we
will be more likely to obtain holiness. It can be so difficult to
be patient with oneself but our Lord is patient with us so we
must follow His example.

Jesus brought me back into the park, near the flower garden.
The priest is out of the mist. (I asked Jesus. I knew Jesus would
move him out fast. I could feel the softness in His heart.) The
man in the boat appeared to be asleep and I asked our Lord if
he was resting. Jesus said he was resting in God, becoming
comfortable with God. Jesus said, *"By the time you are
finished with this visit, he will be in heaven."*

Jesus began to talk about His mercy and those who promote
His mercy. He brought me to a woman who had spread His
mercy on earth. Jesus explained that it is important to talk
about His great mercy, but it is also important to show His
mercy through our actions and even our thoughts. We must be
non-judgmental of others. We must strive to be tolerant and
kind because Jesus is tolerant and kind. If we show mercy to
others, clearly it will be shown to us.

This woman I saw in the mist was so lovable. I felt a great
happiness in being near her. I understood that others on earth
had loved her very much. She had glasses and I understood
that she died near the age of sixty-six years old. She was light-
hearted. Jesus cherished this woman. I could feel it. He had
warmth and tenderness and, I have to say, delight when He
said to me, *"Listen to her. Listen to her prayers."*

She cheerfully thanked Jesus for everything and everyone.

She thanked Him for His mercy to her family, to her friends, to everyone at her job in a school where she worked. She thanked Him for His mercy to herself and to the world. She repeatedly thanked Him for everything under the sun and beyond. This woman did not care at all where she was. The mist was just fine in that she took no notice of her progress or lack of. She remembered all of her friends and their little ailments, their children's difficulties, their fears. She was detached from herself so much on earth that this purgatory experience was just more of the same in that she prayed on earth and now she was praying here.

I looked at Jesus and said, "Why is she here, Lord? She sounds like a saint."

Jesus replied lightly, ***"She had an addiction and she is separating from it. Anne, what is different about the mist around her?"***

I looked and saw that the mist was moving quickly past her. Some souls are in a mist where there is no movement. Others rest in a mist where there is slow, gentle movement. The mist here seemed to be flying past this soul, not that she cared. She took no notice at all because she was so concerned with getting all the graces she could for other souls. Soon, as we watched, Jesus spoke to her.

"Rise, My beloved."

This woman opened her eyes in the light of the park and stood up with complete confidence and joy. After a lovely smile in our direction, she spied a group and immediately made her way to them. This was the funniest experience because she accepted her lightning fast move through this merciful mist as her due, as completely consistent with her expectations. This was how she understood Christ to be, merciful. She expected no less.

Jesus laughed. I laughed too, in plain joy. I said, "Lord,

how could You do anything else?"

Jesus said, *"Exactly, little Anne. How could I do anything else? This soul and all like her disarm Me with their trust. My heart has no protection, no armor against souls such as this. She is so convinced of My goodness and of My mercy, that she comes to the Kingdom in delight. I, in turn, experience delight in her. I cannot help but give her all she requests. While she served on earth, I answered her prayers with great generosity. She trusts Me, Anne. Her trust is a balm to My wounded heart. When I experience man's ingratitude, I look to souls such as this to console Me. She told others about My mercy, she showed others My mercy, and when she died in her body, she experienced My mercy, as you have just seen. Anne, this woman did not judge others. She talked about Me as a loving and merciful God. She was entitled to every bit of mercy she received. Tell all souls that they should talk about My mercy, practice My mercy toward others, and when they come to Me, they will experience My mercy themselves. As you have seen, I cannot resist a soul such as this."*

This was a great joy. Jesus was so happy with this woman. It made me happy to see Him so happy. This woman is a delight to our Jesus and I hope we can all become like her. How willing our Lord is to overlook our flaws if we love and accept His love. I must tell my reader that even now I find I cannot wipe the smile from my face.

I knew it was time to go. I glanced over to the lake and saw the little boat at the shore, waiting for another soul. My unknown friend has gone to heaven.

Part Four

Monthly Messages from Jesus Christ

Jesus

December 1, 2004

"I send graces down upon your world. Indeed, at this time, I begin to flood the world with heavenly graces that will heal souls and convert hearts. Dear children of the one true God, your Savior prepares to return. I want each one of you to welcome My return to the world. In order to do that, you must quiet your heart and accept the gift of My divine grace. I hold the greatest acceptance and forgiveness for you all. My heart bursts with the love I have for you all, and I am returning to reclaim you all. Children of heaven, feel My joy. The time of desolation for souls is at end. I am returning."

God the Father

January 1, 2005

"Dear children of the world, I will never leave you. Please consider me the very best of Fathers. Does a loving father know when his child's heart is grieving? Of course he does. If your heart is grieving, you must come to Me. I will heal your hurts and restore your heart to you. I will give

you courage and strength so that you can proceed with your earthly journey. I am asking you today, though, to proceed differently. Ask Me to be united to you. In this way, you will come to walk on the path that I, through Jesus Christ, have marked out for you. Dearest children of the world, please walk with Me. I need your help. I, the Almighty God, ask you now to walk with Me. There are many souls crying out to Me in pain. You must bring Me to them. My dear ones, bring Me to them."

Jesus

February 1, 2005

"I wish to tell the world of My love. Dearest children of God, you will be welcomed in heaven. You have a family here who prepares for your arrival. Each soul on earth is steadily making progress in their earthly journey in that you are all steadily approaching the end of your life, even if you will live to a very old age. If we begin with that thought, My next thought will make even more sense to you. I wish you to consider what it is you will bring Me when I come for you. Will you bring Me kindness to others? Will you bring Me service to your family? Will you bring Me a duty fulfilled in obedience and dignity? You see, little souls, I will not ask you for your

material possessions because they will have no value here, unless you use these possessions to help others. Only then can material possessions acquire heavenly value. I have placed you in the world to serve. I am with you in each day but you must also be with Me. Dearest children, ask Me for guidance and I will tell you how I wish you to serve."

Jesus

March 1, 2005

"My children are distracted in this time. I am sending great peace upon those who allow Me into their souls, and I wish to be present in every soul. Do you want My heavenly peace? Do you wish to experience a foretaste of heaven? Dear souls, this is available to you if you ask Me. This is not something you can buy. It is not something that the world creates. It is a state of union with Me. It is the experience of being part of the family of God. Each of you belongs to this family, but some of our brothers and sisters have chosen to move away from Me. This results in isolation and sadness. Confusion soon creeps into the life away from God and the soul then seeks to clarify his existence by searching through the worldly balms offered by the enemy. Alas, none of these balms will satisfy a child of heaven because

there is only one true balm for the soul. It is I, Jesus Christ. I am the balm that will heal. I am the balm that will clarify and soothe. I will come to any soul who seeks Me and bring with Me the heavenly peace that cannot be bought. Little children of the world, call out to Me and I will come to you. Confusion is not from Me. Sadness and despair are not from Me. Peace and serenity are from Me. Ask Me to bring these things to you and I will do so."

Jesus

April 1, 2005

"My brothers and sisters, do not be afraid. I have prepared your souls for change. If a teacher prepares a student for an exam, the student should then anticipate the exam with peace, understanding that all that is necessary is steady labor. My brothers and sisters in the world are in a similar position. I have explained through many sources that there are changes coming in the world. I have made it clear that I am overseeing each detail. Each of you, My beloved ones, has a role to play in the time of transition. Look ahead with great peace and courage and you will serve honorably. If the world responds with excitement or distress, you respond with a calm that is noticeable. In

everything, trust Me. Begin today. Regardless of what occurs in your life, respond peacefully, saying often, 'Jesus I trust in You.' I have prepared an army of peaceful soldiers to respond to the changes in this troubled world. You will stand out, My friends. You will spread My peace to every corner. Be joyful as your Jesus is joyful, for truly, the darkness is lifting."

Jesus

May 1, 2005

"Be at peace, dear children of heaven. There is no reason for anything but a peaceful countenance. I am working in your soul if you are allowing Me to do so and you will come closer and closer to Me. You see that I am calling you to do this. I want you to behave like Me and even to think like Me. You will be gentle and kind to those you meet in your day. They will then consider what it is that makes you different. And there is a contrast between those following Me and those following the world. The closer you come to Me, the greater the contrast. I would like to see a multitude of souls drawing closer to Me. You can help with this project because you represent Me. I am calling everyone and I use each of you to do this. So be My voice in your world and cry out to your brothers and sisters.

Tell them of My love for them and tell them of My wish to draw them closer to Me. If you allow Me to work through you, I will do so. If you practice loving all souls and being merciful to all souls, soon you will be speaking My name to them. You understand that if you are not merciful and kind, it will not matter what you say because souls will be repelled. It is only through your love, inspired by Me, that they are moved. So be as gentle as I am gentle and souls will be drawn back into the safe pasture of My Sacred Heart."

Jesus

June 1, 2005

"My brothers and sisters, how I love you. How eager I am that you use the graces available to you. When a soul understands this mission and begins to ask for graces for others, heaven is joyful. In the same way, those on earth who are interceded for begin to benefit and change. Graces surround them. Their souls become alert because there is hope. Dear ones, help Me. I want every soul to return to Me. I am waiting for each soul to become open so that My graces can flood that soul. Many of you have seen this and you understand. For those of you who have not seen this happen, please, ask Me for graces for a soul who is far from Me. Continue asking Me. Ask Me

for graces for strangers. I will come to them in a special way. I will observe them closely, as only I can, given My knowledge of them, and I will find the perfect moment. While I wait for this moment, I will be allowing them to benefit from your prayers and wishes by sending moments of grace and people of grace into their lives. Think, My friends. Did I not do this for you at some time in your life? Did I not pursue you if you were far away? If you were never far away, perhaps I encouraged you when you felt abandoned or afraid. I have graces for each soul in darkness. Please, work for Me now and you will see souls returning. All is well, My dear friends. You are children of heaven and as children of heaven, you have nothing to fear. There is only good possible for you. The earth is a temporary residence. Your home is in heaven, so when you come here, you will have come home. Be joyful servants of your Returning King and you will see great changes in your world."

Jesus

July 1, 2005

"Today I cry out to young people. Young souls are the cherished jewels in the Kingdom of God on earth. The formation of these souls must be treated with reverence. Each individual in the

Kingdom bears a responsibility to young souls, even if it is simply through setting an example of Christian living. Dear children of God, you are accountable for the impact of your actions and each sin carries an impact, however unnoticeable. Search your life and you will discover where I am asking you to assist young people. Many children live in families lacking a parent. Perhaps I am asking you to share your Christianity with those children in order to be a role model. Dear souls, in most cases, young people learn how to be adults by watching others. So your life, the model of your living out your walk with Me, has impact. Your life can be something which a child can measure sin against. Think of a holy person you knew while you were growing up. Now remember back to a time when you saw others committing acts that were unholy. Did you not recognize that these acts would not be acceptable to this holy person? Sometimes it is simply speech. There are certain people near whom you will be careful about what you say. I am asking you to be one of those people. I want others to take note of your presence and know that Jesus should not be insulted. I want others to understand that your Church should not be unjustly vilified in your presence. In short, I want others to know that when you are present, I am present. They will then use you as the standard against which they measure their actions. You must stand for Me. I am asking each of you to sit in silence and consider how I am asking you to assist My young people in the world. Be assured of My great gratitude in this matter.

Through this mission of mercy and love I wish to call all young people back to My heart. Will you help Me?"

Jesus

August 1, 2005

"Listen to your Savior, My dear ones. I am speaking to every soul on earth at this time. I am with you in each moment and I will never leave you. You must accept each experience in union with Me. You will have difficulties if you begin to follow me but you have had difficulties in the past. I do not wish My apostles to believe that life without service to Me would mean life without difficulties. If the cross is weighing you down, bring it to Me. I am the Expert at carrying the cross. It is understandable that you will need help with your difficulties and it is only sensible to come to the Expert for that help. This is a sensible approach to living your life and carrying your cross. Together, we will continue on. You will support Me in My mission of mercy, and I will support you in everything. The benefits of service to heaven are complete. There nothing you lack when you serve heaven because heaven knows your every need. You offer Me your day each morning. Be aware that this act is mutual. When you give Me your day, I am allowed

*into that day and I walk through each moment
with you, flowing through you, yes, but also
caring for you, alerting you to danger, and
insuring that your soul benefits from each
challenge, each joy, each cross. You are not alone.
I will not allow anything for you that I will not
use for your ultimate holiness. Walk in joy
because as an apostle serving in this troubled
world, you are entitled to every heavenly
protection. My gratitude to you for your
friendship is not something you can measure in
earthly terms. You must trust Me that My
gratitude will astound you. I care for your loved
ones, dear apostles. I hear your prayers and I will
use a measure of My gratitude to you for the
benefit of all of your intentions for other souls.
There is no reason, whatever your circumstances,
to lose your joy."*

Jesus

September 1, 2005

*"God's little children know great suffering on
earth, it is true. There will always be those who
are suffering. Extend the greatest love and
assistance to those who carry the cross because
you will carry it one day and you will then benefit
from the help of others. Dear brothers and
sisters, all is well. I can say that all is well*

because I view all from the perspective of heaven. Can I ask you to share that view with Me? I will give you this view if you are willing to accept it. From heaven I see the souls cry out to Me. They ask for a relief from darkness. I am sending relief, My dear faithful ones. I am sending great conversion graces. There are times when a child is having trouble and the child cannot see how to solve a problem or remove himself from a situation. The parent sees more clearly, of course, and often understands what the child needs to recover. What parent is unfamiliar with the protesting cry of the child who wants to do it his own way, despite the danger of the child's intended path? The parent must then step in and avert the child's course, showing the child the better and safer way. Such protests a parent must endure. But a good parent perseveres in the course that will benefit the child in the long run. I am the Parent in this time. I am looking at the world and I have decided that it is time to pierce the darkness with My light. I have told this to My beloved apostles. Please trust Me. Please do as I ask and examine your role in the renewal each morning, when you offer Me your day. I will then continue to flow My light through you into the world. Dearest friends, I am your Savior. I do not abandon you. Do you understand that heaven is your intended destination? Do not object when others come to heaven. It is for this they were born on this earth. I understand earthly grief. You know that I understand because I experienced great human grieving on earth. I

*will comfort you. I will sustain you. You have
been asked to spread My heavenly calm. All is
well. You know this because I am telling you this.
You are one who believes your God. Spread My
calm, My grace, My joy. Will you support your
Jesus in everything? It is this I am asking of you.
Rest joyfully in your soul with Me. I will give you
exactly what is needed for your world and you
will be a holy carrier of My grace. I am with you.
Rejoice."*

Jesus

October 1, 2005

*"I have willed a great time of joy for My beloved
apostles. Joy is something that the world wishes
to take from God's children, but joy is available
nonetheless. The world encourages souls to
concentrate on comfort and earthly possessions. I
ask you to concentrate on service. This is a
marked contrast, is it not? Let Me explain why
concentrating on service brings you joy. If you rise
each day and pledge allegiance to God, you will
begin that day with more thought of serving than
being served. In this way you look at your day as
an opportunity to work for heaven and to work
for heaven's children, your brothers and sisters.
This perspective sends you into the day as a
servant. When the day presents you with the*

inevitable opportunities to assist or console, or simply to be tolerant of your brothers or sisters, you do not view this as a burden, or an interruption in your entertainment and comfort, but as a request made to you directly from the throne of your God. And fulfilling a request made to you by your God brings you joy. You serve heaven and we fulfill our part of the agreement by sending you joy. If all of God's children were living this way, there would be a great joy on earth and through this joy would come peace. This is because an apostle does not become angry when he or she is inconvenienced. That apostle responds in calm trust when the world presents him with difficulty or even pain. There is no striking out at others. There is no rebelliousness. There is peace. The world is changing and it is changing one soul at a time. Join Me now and make a commitment to peace in your world. I will send it through you, My beloved apostles."

Jesus

November 1, 2005

"My apostles will be known by their love. It has always been this way. Look for those who treat others gently and you will see My hand at work. If you begin to follow Me, you will be gentle and loving to others. Dear apostles, during this time

I send you great graces. Everything you need comes from Me. Do not hesitate to answer My call because you feel you are not holy enough. You are called to holiness, it is true, but all genuine holiness comes from Me. If you ask Me I will send it to you in great abundance. I notice that many souls fear a commitment to Me because they see only their flaws and weaknesses. At this time I want you to stop thinking that it is your humanity that gives Me glory. Souls in heaven give Me praise, it is true. And I return their love. But when a soul on earth, acting from faith, makes even the smallest act of love or fidelity to Me, I am given great glory and the family of God is given power. Yes, each time a soul on earth steps out for God in any way, the Kingdom grows. Do not put a limit on the importance of each little act and each little prayer. If you rose each day and pledged your allegiance to heaven with an honest desire to serve, and then went out and committed sins all day, you would still be considered a friend to the Savior. Now I know you will not do this because when you pledge your allegiance to Me, you are then wrapped in great graces. These graces assist you in each moment and illuminate My will for you so that you can more easily make heavenly decisions. But I am making a point so that you will understand that if you try to please Me in even the smallest way, you will change the world. Each prayer, however small and imperfect, fuels this renewal. Will you answer My call? I am relying on My apostles on earth to spread My words and to allow My light and love to flow back into this world. It is only a difficult job if you rely on yourself. If you rely on Me, you will see the greatest things happen in the shortest time. You will be filled with My love for others. Ask Me for this. When you do not feel My love, remind Me of this promise and I will make good on it by sending you great love for others. This prayer always reflects My will and will always be answered. If you see souls through My eyes, you will love them. Be at peace in each moment because you are surrounded by heaven. There is nothing to fear. Let love direct your actions and you will be a part of My heavenly team."

Jesus

December 1, 2005

"Dear children, you were each created by the Father. He takes the greatest joy in watching you progress as you learn how to love during your time in the world. You experience difficulties in this regard but you overcome these difficulties and you grow and advance. This process of learning to love and rejecting all that is not love is the real point of your time on the earth. If you were told that you would be coming to heaven soon, how would you treat the souls around you? How would you treat them differently if you knew

*that your time with each of them was limited?
Well, little souls, I am reminding you today that
your time with each of the souls around you is
finite. Time will pass and your time with that soul
will be over. If you love each soul in your life, you
will be at peace when your time together is
finished. You will feel satisfaction in that you will
know that you tried to love them, despite the
difficulties that arose to make this more
challenging. These difficulties or obstacles to love
originate from two sources. One source of
difficulty is your own failings and the other
source of difficulty is the failings of the other
soul. These difficulties, which are expected, must
be overcome so that you can treat each other with
the pure love that you will experience in heaven.
When you find another soul unlovable, remember
that you will most likely be with that soul in
heaven and you will love each other perfectly
there. It will greatly please and console the
heavenly Father if you begin treating others this
way on earth. If you had to do this alone, you
would surely struggle and find yourself without
the forgiveness necessary to love each other as we
love in heaven. But you do not proceed alone. You
proceed with all of heaven and with Me, Jesus
Christ. I have given you many examples of how I
loved during My time on earth. Read about Me in
Scripture, dear apostles, and then be gentle as I
was gentle. Be kind as I was kind. Be respectful as
I was respectful. Be forgiving as I was forgiving. I
am with you in each moment and you may ask Me
for the grace to love each soul in your life. I will*

send you this grace and together, you and I will prepare you to love like a resident of heaven. In this process you will find great joy. This joy is only the very beginning of My reward to you. Be at peace. Your God created you to love and He will teach you how to do this."

Jesus

January 1, 2006

"My apostles hear My voice and know that their Savior speaks. More and more I will speak to My apostles in their souls, directing their actions. I am returning at this very moment through each one of you. Can a plan be more perfect? Bring others to Me so that I can flow into the world through each one of them, also. Dear friends of the Savior, together we are changing your world. When souls feel fear, we bring them calm. When souls feel anger, we bring them forgiveness. When souls feel abandoned, we bring love. When souls feel great grief, we will bring comfort. And when souls see death, we will bring them to an acceptance of heaven so that they understand eternal life. Many in the world today do not understand their inheritance. This creates a fear of death that prevents souls from living fully. If a soul accepts the truth about

eternity, that soul works for Me because the soul knows that glory only lasts if it is obtained for heaven. The glory of heaven is love and is obtained by how much one loved on earth. Souls will be disappointed when they look back on their life if their life was lived in selfishness and if their purpose in life was to obtain worldly goods. This will be a disappointment for them, for Me, and for their families if their families were led astray by this flawed vision of the purpose of life. If you realign the purpose in your life, I will then help to realign the purpose for each member of your family. This is My promise to you. Make Me, Jesus Christ, the purpose of your life, and I will work through you to claim the world. How can I help the world through you and the life I have given you? How can you set an example so that others will identify Me in you and in your actions? Think on this, My beloved apostle. Meditate on this. Give Me the time to direct your soul because your soul and your life on earth are necessary for My plan. We do not want the Kingdom to lose souls because you lived a flawed purpose. This will not happen, of course, because you are listening to Me. But you must give me the time each day to work in your soul, to communicate with you, to restore the precious calm that is our gift to the world at this time. This becomes more important each day. I send calm to you. You bring it to others. Do not be afraid when you do not feel calm. This simply means that the world has taken your calm and you must come back to Me so that I can give you more. This will work but in order for it to work you must make your commitment to prayer time. Consider today and each day what time is My time. When will you sit in silence so I can communicate with you? If you do not have a set time, perhaps you will set one now. I love you totally. I rely on you, My dearest apostle. I am grateful to you in the extreme and I am blessing your loved ones. I will keep my part of the bargain. Accept the gift of calm in your life and I will direct you in everything. Then your life will be lived for God's purposes and, truly, My Kingdom will come."

Jesus

February 1, 2006

"Dearest apostle, I urge you to be little in your soul. Only in spiritual humility will you see the true state of your soul and so understand the work necessary for you to become holy. Holiness is your target. If a soul is holy, I can flow great graces through that soul into the world. Do not think about your own goals, little apostle, without checking them against My goals. In this time I require many apostles who strive to be humble. This is the opposite of what the world encourages. Do you see? Study this concept and

you will see that great smallness is necessary in the Kingdom of God. Souls in heaven do not tear each other down, but bring each other up. My souls in heaven seek ways to affirm the struggling souls on earth. They do not consider how to put themselves forward, but rather how to best lift a soul towards holiness. You must be the same. I entreat you to listen to your Savior. Strive for smallness in your service to the Kingdom. Be content to allow Me to have the glory. I will gaze into your soul and see the longing for holiness and I will make you holy, but I can only do this if you allow Me. My beloved ones, you will see in My life an example of constant patience with others. I was gentle on earth and I am still gentle. I am patient with you. You must be patient with others. You must be gentle with others. You must be forgiving of others, trusting My ability to work in the soul who allows Me the freedom. If a soul is willing, I will help him. I have told you this. Trust My words and pray for each other, particularly those with whom you are called to walk during this time of transition. Dearest friends of heaven, believe Me when I tell you that all will be well. Your concern at this time should be to advance in holiness and you will only advance if you remain small. Be at peace in everything because My grace is more powerful than any bitter plans of the enemy. I am asking you to concentrate on your own movement to me. For each apostle who gives Me his pride, I give the world My majesty, the majesty of Jesus Christ, your Returning King."

Jesus

March 1, 2006

"Children, My words carry My love for you. When you read My words, understand that I send them to you because I love you. This entire mission is predicated by My love for you. You must consider that I speak words in order to help you accept My love and allow My love to change your heart. Sometimes you listen to what I am saying but do not change your little heart and in this instance My words have not helped you. At other times, you allow these words to minister to your soul and then your little heart can change and soften, filling up with the divine and allowing the divine to direct you. When this happens, when you allow My words and graces to alter the way you think and live, then this mission is a success. The world is changing, dear apostle. You make a decision to sit quietly with Me and listen to My words and that small act insures that the world will change because you are cooperating with Me. My goals for you include only what is best for you and for the world around you. In a time when many seek to direct you to My enemy, I have come to direct you to heaven. This is a mercy, of course, and I know you are grateful. God is consoled by the gratitude of His children. I want you to use this message to take inventory of your priceless little soul. Sit in silence with Me and rest in My perfect

and complete love for you. I accept you, My little treasure, in all of your imperfection. Your sin does not discourage Me in the least. Bring Me your sins. Confess your sins. Please do not think that because of your sins your Jesus could not love you. I do love you, in all of your sin and pain. This mission of love is in existence because I love you. I am speaking to you right now because I love you. Dearest little apostle, you are chosen to work in this world intimately united to Me. Will you say 'yes' to Me? Will you accept My tender and complete love for you and allow Me to soften your little heart? Do not turn Me away. I am your Jesus. I have come for you. Open your heart for Me in the smallest way and I will come to live with you forever. I want only what is good for you and through what is good for you, I will renew the world. Please, accept Me."

Jesus

April 1, 2006

"My apostles seek to please Me. The desire to please your Savior, all by itself, gives Me the greatest consolation. If you have the smallest desire to please Me, little apostle, you can be certain that you have already done so. The desire to please Me is only the beginning, of course. From that desire I move you into active service to the

Kingdom. How badly the Kingdom of God requires steady apostles in this time. I rely most heavily on those who are consistent in their service. My little ones see My plan for them in the present moment. At times My little ones underestimate how I intend to use them in the future. This is acceptable, of course, because it is best if a serving apostle remains focused on the day in which he finds himself. Let Me assure you, though, that the level of service I can gain from you tomorrow and in every tomorrow that I grant you, is directly affected by the level of cooperation I gain from you today. If you serve Me in completeness today, you can be assured that I am preparing you for even greater service tomorrow. It is all about practice, after all. You must practice being holy. My dear friends, My apostles, do not be afraid of tomorrow, regardless of what occurs today. My plan is detailed and accounts for everything. I will care for My beloved friends and their loved ones. I am God. I am all-powerful. You cannot place too much trust in Me because I will always outperform your greatest expectations. Serve completely in today, My friends, and I will use you even more effectively tomorrow. Trust your Jesus. I will protect you."

Jesus

May 1, 2006

"My friends in the world know suffering. This will not change and it has always been this way. What separates My friends from those who walk without Me is the grace that accompanies My followers. If a soul is willing to accept heavenly grace, that soul's suffering is changed. Crosses carried in union with heaven benefit both the individual soul and the world. When viewed this way, which is the true way, souls understand that suffering is not a bad thing, but a valuable thing to be exploited for heaven. Do not think that your Jesus misunderstands the difficulty associated with suffering. Always consider the suffering I accepted in the world, on the cross in My final hours, of course, but also throughout My life. I did not spend time on earth in comfort and leisure. I worked hard each day and often did without things that souls today take for granted. Consider My life on earth in its entirety. Dearest apostle, My friend, I lived as quietly as possible. I prayed for you each day. I offered comfort and assistance to others in pain or need. I committed Myself to My duty each day and never deviated from My responsibilities. I did this because I knew that you would benefit from a model to follow. You see, I spent each day on earth aware of your life. When I was tempted to become disheartened, I thought of you, struggling, and I

*disciplined Myself to be brave and hopeful. I
offered My struggles to God the Father and asked
that, in return, He grant you graces of courage
and hope. I did not waste any time on earth, My
beloved. Please think often of My life on earth
and understand that I thought of you each day
and set an example for you on each day. If you
remember this, that I walked the earth for you,
you will understand that you walk on earth with
Me, Someone who understands your every fear,
your every temptation. Be at peace. Let us walk
together. Time cannot separate an apostle from
his Savior. Again and always I assure you, I am
with you."*

Jesus

June 1, 2006

*"I speak to My beloved apostles today from the
pain of My wounded heart. I suffer for each soul
walking the earth without knowledge of My love.
Despite rejection, My love cannot be limited and
overflows into the world. Those who do not
welcome the love of the Savior continue in
loneliness. Those who welcome My love are
deluged with it. Dear apostles, I know that you
are weary. You do not see the full impact of your
service on the Kingdom but please believe that
one day you will experience the fruits of your*

labor. You will exult in each act of service and each act of self-denial because you will see the act attached to all of the graces obtained from it. At that time you will marvel at My generosity. You will also thank Me for obscuring this from you during your time of service because it is through this trust that you gain both merit for your eternity and conversion graces for souls. How many sinners are pulled back into My Sacred Heart through your smallest act of trust and love in the face of scorn and mockery? Dear apostles, you must consider whether or not you yourself were called back to Me through the selfless action of another. It is in this way that we are a family. Each apostle is indebted to others for his progress up the mountain of holiness because the service of each supports and sustains others. How blessed is the plan of God. My gratitude to you will endure forever. Continue on in service to the Kingdom and you will see yourself counted as My friend and loyal follower. Imagine My gratitude. The enemy taunts God, stating that God's children have turned their faces away from heaven. The enemy boasts that God's children are listening to the voice of darkness. During all of this, the apostles of Jesus Christ remain steadfast. Your faces are turned to heaven and you listen to My voice. Pay no attention to the empty words of the enemy, My beloved ones. Let My voice console you and direct you and you will not be deceived. Work for souls, so that they will accept My love. All is well. I am with you in each moment."

Appendix

Guidelines for Lay Apostles

As lay apostles of Jesus Christ the Returning King, we agree to perform our basic obligations as practicing Catholics. Additionally, we will adopt the following spiritual practices, as best we can:

1. **Allegiance Prayer** and **Morning Offering**, plus a brief prayer for the Holy Father
2. **Eucharistic Adoration**, one hour per week
3. **Prayer Group Participation**, monthly, at which we pray the Luminous Mysteries of the Holy Rosary and read the Monthly Message
4. **Monthly Confession**
5. Further, we will follow the example of Jesus Christ as set out in the Holy Scripture, treating all others with His patience and kindness.

Allegiance Prayer

Dear God in heaven, I pledge my allegiance to You. I give You my life, my work and my heart. In turn, give me the grace of obeying Your every direction to the fullest possible extent. Amen.

Morning Offering

O Jesus, through the Immaculate Heart of Mary, I offer You the prayers, works, joys and sufferings of this day, for all the intentions of Your Sacred Heart, in union with the Holy Sacrifice of the Mass throughout the world, in reparation for my sins, and for the intentions of the Holy Father. Amen.

Prayer for the Holy Father

Blessed Mother of Jesus, protect our Holy Father, Benedict XVI, and bless his intentions.

Five Luminous Mysteries

1. The Baptism of Jesus
2. The Wedding at Cana
3. The Proclamation of the Kingdom of God
4. The Transfiguration
5. The Institution of the Eucharist

Promise from Jesus to His Lay Apostles

May 12, 2005

Your message to souls remains constant. Welcome each soul to the rescue mission. You may assure each lay apostle that just as they concern themselves with My interests, I will concern Myself with theirs. They will be placed in My Sacred Heart and I will defend and protect them. I will also pursue complete conversion of each of their loved ones. So you see, the souls who serve in this rescue mission as My beloved lay apostles will know peace. The world cannot make this promise as only heaven can bestow peace on a soul. This is truly heaven's mission and I call every one of heaven's children to assist Me. You will be well rewarded, My dear ones.

Prayers Taken from The Volumes

Prayers to God the Father

"I trust You, God. I offer You my pain in the spirit of acceptance and I will serve You in every circumstance."

"God my Father in heaven, You are all mercy. You love me and see my every sin. God, I call on You now as the Merciful Father. Forgive my every sin. Wash away the stains on my soul so that I may once again rest in complete innocence. I trust You, Father in heaven. I rely on You. I thank You. Amen."

"God my Father, calm my spirit and direct my path."

"God, I have made mistakes. I am sorry. I am Your child, though, and seek to be united to You."

"I believe in God. I believe Jesus is calling me. I believe my Blessed Mother has requested my help. Therefore I am going to pray on this day and every day."

"God my Father, help me to understand."

Prayers to Jesus

"Jesus, I give You my day."

"Jesus, how do You want to use me on this day? You have a willing servant in me, Jesus. Allow me to work for the Kingdom."

"Lord, what can I do today to prepare for Your coming? Direct me, Lord, and I will see to Your wishes."

"Lord, help me."

"Jesus, love me."

Prayers to the Angels

"Angels from heaven, direct my path."

"Dearest angel guardian, I desire to serve Jesus by remaining at peace. Please obtain for me the graces necessary to maintain His divine peace in my heart."

Prayers for a Struggling Soul

"Jesus, what do You think of all this? Jesus, what do You want me to do for this soul? Jesus, show me how to bring You into this situation."

"Angel guardian, thank you for your constant vigil over this soul. Saints in heaven, please assist this dear angel."

Prayers for Children

"God in heaven, You are the Creator of all things. Please send Your graces down upon our world."

"Jesus, I love You."

"Jesus, I trust in You. Jesus, I trust in You. Jesus, I trust in You."

"Jesus, I offer You my day."

"Mother Mary, help me to be good."

How to Recite the Chaplet of Divine Mercy

The Chaplet of Mercy is recited using ordinary Rosary beads of five decades. The Chaplet is preceded by two opening prayers from the *Diary* of Saint Faustina and followed by a closing prayer.

1. Make the Sign of the Cross

In the name of the Father, and of the Son, and of the Holy Spirit. Amen.

2. Optional Opening Prayers

You expired, Jesus, but the source of life gushed forth for souls, and the ocean of mercy opened up for the whole world. O Fount of Life, unfathomable Divine Mercy, envelop the whole world and empty Yourself out upon us.

O Blood and Water, which gushed forth from the Heart of Jesus as a fountain of mercy for us, I trust in You!

3. Our Father

Our Father, who art in heaven, hallowed be Thy name. Thy kingdom come. Thy will be done on earth as it is in heaven. Give us this day our daily bread. And forgive us our trespasses, as we forgive those who trespass against us. And lead us not into temptation, but deliver us from evil. Amen.

4. Hail Mary

Hail Mary, full of grace, the Lord is with thee. Blessed art thou among women, and blessed is the fruit of thy womb, Jesus. Holy Mary, Mother of God, pray for us sinners, now and at the hour of our death. Amen.

5. The Apostles' Creed

I believe in God, the Father Almighty, Creator of heaven and earth. I believe in Jesus Christ, His only Son, Our Lord. He was conceived by the power of the Holy Spirit and born of the Virgin Mary. He suffered under Pontius Pilate, was crucified, died, and was buried. He descended to the dead. On the third day He rose again. He ascended into heaven, and is seated at the right hand of the Father. He will come again to judge the living and the dead. I believe in the Holy Spirit, the holy Catholic Church, the Communion of Saints, the forgiveness of sins, the resurrection of the body, and life everlasting. Amen.

6. The Eternal Father

Eternal Father, I offer You the Body and Blood, Soul and Divinity of Your Dearly Beloved Son, Our Lord, Jesus Christ, in atonement for our sins and those of the whole world.

7. On the Ten Small Beads of Each Decade

For the sake of His Sorrowful Passion, have mercy on us and on the whole world.

8. Repeat for the remaining decades

Saying the "Eternal Father" (6) on the "Our Father" bead and then 10 "For the sake of His Sorrowful Passion" (7) on the following "Hail Mary" beads.

9. Conclude with Holy God

Holy God, Holy Mighty One, Holy Immortal One, have mercy on us and on the whole world.

10. Optional Closing Prayer

Eternal God, in whom mercy is endless and the treasury of compassion—inexhaustible, look kindly upon us and increase Your mercy in us, that in difficult moments we might not despair nor become despondent, but with great confidence submit ourselves to Your holy will, which is Love and Mercy itself.

To learn more about the image of The Divine Mercy, the Chaplet of Divine Mercy and the series of revelations given to St. Faustina Kowalska please contact:

Marians of the Immaculate Conception
Stockbridge, Massachusetts 01263
Telephone 800-462-7426
www.marian.org

How to Pray the Rosary

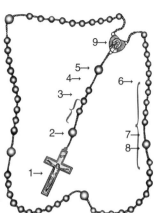

1. Make the Sign of the Cross and say the "Apostles Creed."
2. Say the "Our Father."
3. Say three "Hail Marys."
4. Say the "Glory be to the Father."
5. Announce the First Mystery; then say the "Our Father."
6. Say ten "Hail Marys," while meditating on the Mystery.
7. Say the "Glory be to the Father." After each decade say the following prayer requested by the Blessed Virgin Mary at Fatima: "O my Jesus, forgive us our sins, save us from the fires of hell, lead all souls to Heaven, especially those in most need of Thy mercy."
8. Announce the Second Mystery: then say the "Our Father." Repeat 6 and 7 and continue with the Third, Fourth, and Fifth Mysteries in the same manner.
9. Say the "Hail, Holy Queen" on the medal after the five decades are completed.

As a general rule, depending on the season, the Joyful Mysteries are said on Monday and Saturday; the Sorrowful Mysteries on Tuesday and Friday; the Glorious Mysteries on Wednesday and Sunday; and the Luminous Mysteries on Thursday.

Papal Reflections of the Mysteries

The Joyful Mysteries

The Joyful Mysteries are marked by the joy radiating from the event of the Incarnation. This is clear from the very first mystery, the Annunciation, where Gabriel's greeting to the Virgin of Nazareth is linked to an invitation to messianic joy: "Rejoice, Mary." The whole of salvation... had led up to this greeting.

(Prayed on Mondays and Saturdays, and optional on Sundays during Advent and the Christmas Season.)

The Luminous Mysteries

Moving on from the infancy and the hidden life in Nazareth to the public life of Jesus, our contemplation brings us to those mysteries which may be called in a special way "mysteries of light." Certainly, the whole mystery of Christ is a mystery of light. He is the "Light of the world" (John 8:12). Yet this truth emerges in a special way during the years of His public life. (Prayed on Thursdays.)

The Sorrowful Mysteries

The Gospels give great prominence to the Sorrowful Mysteries of Christ. From the beginning, Christian piety, especially during the Lenten devotion of the Way of the Cross, has focused on the individual moments of the Passion, realizing that here is found the culmination of the revelation of God's love and the source of our salvation. (Prayed on Tuesdays and Fridays, and optional on Sundays during Lent.)

The Glorious Mysteries

"The contemplation of Christ's face cannot stop at the image of the Crucified One. He is the Risen One!" The Rosary has always expressed this knowledge born of faith and invited the believer to pass beyond the darkness of the Passion in order to gaze upon Christ's glory in the Resurrection and Ascension... Mary herself would be raised to that same glory in the Assumption. (Prayed on Wednesdays and Sundays.)

From the *Apostolic Letter The Rosary of the Virgin Mary*, Pope John Paul II, Oct. 16, 2002.

Prayers of the Rosary

The Sign of the Cross

In the name of the Father, and of the Son, and of the Holy Spirit. Amen.

The Apostles' Creed

I believe in God, the Father Almighty, Creator of heaven and earth. I believe in Jesus Christ, His only Son, Our Lord. He was conceived by the power of the Holy Spirit and born of the Virgin Mary. He suffered under Pontius Pilate, was crucified, died, and was buried. He descended to the dead. On the third day He rose again. He ascended into heaven, and is seated at the right hand of the Father. He will come again to judge the living and the dead. I believe in the Holy Spirit, the holy Catholic Church, the Communion of Saints, the forgiveness of sins, the resurrection of the body, and life everlasting. Amen.

Our Father

Our Father, who art in heaven, hallowed be Thy name. Thy kingdom come. Thy will be done on earth as it is in heaven. Give us this day our daily bread. And forgive us our trespasses, as we forgive those who trespass against us. And lead us not into temptation, but deliver us from evil. Amen.

Hail Mary

Hail Mary, full of grace, the Lord is with thee. Blessed art thou among women, and blessed is the fruit of thy womb, Jesus. Holy Mary, Mother of God, pray for us sinners, now and at the hour of our death. Amen.

Glory Be to the Father

Glory be to the Father, and to the Son, and to the Holy Spirit. As it was in the beginning, is now, and ever shall be, world without end. Amen.

Hail Holy Queen

Hail, Holy Queen, Mother of Mercy, our life, our sweetness and
our hope. To thee do we cry, poor banished children of Eve. To
thee do we send up our sighs, mourning and weeping in this
valley of tears. Turn then, most gracious Advocate, thine eyes of
mercy towards us. And after this, our exile, show unto us the
blessed fruit of thy womb, Jesus. O clement, O loving, O sweet
Virgin Mary!

Pray for us, O Holy Mother of God.
That we may be made worthy of the promises of Christ.

The Mysteries

First Joyful Mystery:
The Annunciation

And when the angel had come to her, he said, "Hail, full of grace,
the Lord is with thee. Blessed art thou among women."

(Luke 1:28)

One Our Father, Ten Hail Marys,
One Glory Be, etc.

Fruit of the Mystery: ***Humility***

Second Joyful Mystery:
The Visitation

Elizabeth was filled with the Holy Spirit and cried out in a loud
voice: "Blest are you among women and blest is the fruit of your
womb."   (*Luke* 1:41-42)

One Our Father, Ten Hail Marys,
One Glory Be, etc.

Fruit of the Mystery: ***Love of Neighbor***

Third Joyful Mystery:
The Birth of Jesus

She gave birth to her first-born Son and wrapped Him in swaddling clothes and laid Him in a manger, because there was no room for them in the place where travelers lodged.   (*Luke* 2:7)

One *Our Father*, Ten *Hail Marys*,
One *Glory Be*, etc.

Fruit of the Mystery: ***Poverty***

Fourth Joyful Mystery:
The Presentation

When the day came to purify them according to the law of Moses, the couple brought Him up to Jerusalem so that He could be presented to the Lord, for it is written in the law of the Lord, "Every first-born male shall be consecrated to the Lord."
(*Luke* 2:22-23)

One *Our Father*, Ten *Hail Marys*,
One *Glory Be*, etc.

Fruit of the Mystery: ***Obedience***

Fifth Joyful Mystery:
The Finding of the Child Jesus in the Temple

On the third day they came upon Him in the temple sitting in the midst of the teachers, listening to them and asking them questions.   (*Luke* 2:46)

One *Our Father*, Ten *Hail Marys*,
One *Glory Be*, etc.

Fruit of the Mystery: ***Joy in Finding Jesus***

First Luminous Mystery:
The Baptism of Jesus

And when Jesus was baptized... the heavens were opened and He saw the Spirit of God descending like a dove, and alighting on Him, and lo, a voice from heaven, saying "this is My beloved Son," with whom I am well pleased."   (*Matthew* 3:16-17)

One *Our Father*, Ten *Hail Marys*,
One *Glory Be*, etc.

Fruit of the Mystery: ***Openness to the Holy Spirit***

Second Luminous Mystery:
The Wedding at Cana

His mother said to the servants, "Do whatever He tells you." . . . Jesus said to them, "Fill the jars with water." And they filled them up to the brim.

(John 2:5-7)

One *Our Father*, Ten *Hail Marys*,
One *Glory Be*, etc.

Fruit of the Mystery: ***To Jesus through Mary***

Third Luminous Mystery:
The Proclamation of the Kingdom of God

"And preach as you go, saying, 'The kingdom of heaven is at hand.' Heal the sick, raise the dead, cleanse lepers, cast out demons. You received without pay, give without pay."

(Matthew 10:7-8)

One *Our Father*, Ten *Hail Marys*,
One *Glory Be*, etc.

Fruit of the Mystery: ***Repentance and Trust in God***

Fourth Luminous Mystery:
The Transfiguration

And as He was praying, the appearance of His countenance was altered and His raiment become dazzling white. And a voice came out of the cloud saying, "This is My Son, My chosen; listen to Him!

(Luke 9:29, 35)

One *Our Father*, Ten *Hail Marys*,
One *Glory Be*, etc.

Fruit of the Mystery: ***Desire for Holiness***

Fifth Luminous Mystery:
The Institution of the Eucharist

And He took bread, and when He had given thanks He broke it and gave it to them, saying, "This is My body which is given for you." . . . And likewise the cup after supper, saying, "This cup which is poured out for you is the new covenant in My blood."

(Luke 22:19-20)

One *Our Father*, Ten *Hail Marys*,
One *Glory Be*, etc.

Fruit of the Mystery: ***Adoration***

First Sorrowful Mystery:
The Agony in the Garden

In His anguish He prayed with all the greater intensity, and His sweat became like drops of blood falling to the ground. Then He rose from prayer and came to His disciples, only to find them asleep, exhausted with grief. (*Luke* 22:44-45)

One *Our Father*, Ten *Hail Marys*,
One *Glory Be*, etc.

Fruit of the Mystery: ***Sorrow for Sin***

Second Sorrowful Mystery:
The Scourging at the Pillar

Pilate's next move was to take Jesus and have Him scourged.

(*John* 19:1)

One *Our Father*, Ten *Hail Marys*,
One *Glory Be*, etc.

Fruit of the Mystery: ***Purity***

Third Sorrowful Mystery:
The Crowning with Thorns

They stripped off His clothes and wrapped Him in a scarlet military cloak. Weaving a crown out of thorns they fixed it on His head, and stuck a reed in His right hand... (Matthew 27:28-29)

One *Our Father*, Ten *Hail Marys*,
One *Glory Be*, etc.

Fruit of the Mystery: ***Courage***

Fourth Sorrowful Mystery:
The Carrying of the Cross

… carrying the cross by Himself, He went out to what is called the Place of the Skull (in Hebrew, Golgotha).   (*John* 19:17)

> One *Our Father*, Ten *Hail Marys*,
> One *Glory Be*, etc.

Fruit of the Mystery: ***Patience***

Fifth Sorrowful Mystery:
The Crucifixion

Jesus uttered a loud cry and said, "Father, into Your hands I commend My spirit." After He said this, He expired.(*L u k e* 23:46)

> One *Our Father*, Ten *Hail Marys*,
> One *Glory Be*, etc.

Fruit of the Mystery: ***Perseverance***

First Glorious Mystery:
The Resurrection

You need not be amazed! You are looking for Jesus of Nazareth, the one who was crucified. He has been raised up; He is not here. See the place where they laid Him."   (*Mark* 16:6)

> One *Our Father*, Ten *Hail Marys*,
> One *Glory Be*, etc.

Fruit of the Mystery: ***Faith***

Second Glorious Mystery:
The Ascension

Then, after speaking to them, the Lord Jesus was taken up into Heaven and took His seat at God's right hand.   (*Mark* 16:19)

> One *Our Father*, Ten *Hail Marys*,
> One *Glory Be*, etc.

Fruit of the Mystery: ***Hope***

Third Glorious Mystery:
The Descent of the Holy Spirit

All were filled with the Holy Spirit. They began to express themselves in foreign tongues and make bold proclamation as the Spirit prompted them. (*Acts* 2:4)

One *Our Father*, Ten *Hail Marys*,
One *Glory Be*, etc.

Fruit of the Mystery: ***Love of God***

Fourth Glorious Mystery:
The Assumption

You are the glory of Jerusalem... you are the splendid boast of our people... God is pleased with what you have wrought. May you be blessed by the Lord Almighty forever and ever.

(*Judith* 15:9-10)

One *Our Father*, Ten *Hail Marys*,
One *Glory Be*, etc.

Fruit of the Mystery: ***Grace of a Happy Death***

Fifth Glorious Mystery:
The Coronation

A great sign appeared in the sky, a woman clothed with the sun, with the moon under her feet, and on her head a crown of twelve stars. (*Revelation* 12:1)

One *Our Father*, Ten *Hail Marys*,
One *Glory Be*, etc.

Fruit of the Mystery: ***Trust in Mary's Intercession***

The Volumes

Direction for Our Times
as given to Anne, a lay apostle

Volume One:	***Thoughts on Spirituality***
Volume Two:	***Conversations with the***
	Eucharistic Heart of Jesus
Volume Three:	***God the Father Speaks to***
	His Children
	The Blessed Mother Speaks
	to Her Bishops and Priests
Volume Four:	***Jesus the King***
	Heaven Speaks to Priests
	Jesus Speaks to Sinners
Volume Six:	***Heaven Speaks to Families***
Volume Seven:	***Greetings from Heaven***
Volume Nine:	***Angels***
Volume Ten:	***Jesus Speaks to His Apostles***

Volumes 5 and 8 will be printed at a later date.

The Volumes are now available in PDF format
for free download and printing from our website:
www.directionforourtimes.org.
We encourage everyone to print and distribute them.

The Volumes are also available at your local bookstore.

The "Heaven Speaks" Booklets
Direction for Our Times
as given to Anne, a lay apostle

The following booklets are available individually from
Direction for Our Times:

Heaven Speaks About Abortion
Heaven Speaks About Addictions
Heaven Speaks to Victims of Clerical Abuse
Heaven Speaks to Consecrated Souls
Heaven Speaks About Depression
Heaven Speaks About Divorce
Heaven Speaks to Prisoners
Heaven Speaks to Soldiers
Heaven Speaks About Stress
Heaven Speaks to Young Adults

Heaven Speaks to Those Away from the Church
Heaven Speaks to Those Considering Suicide
Heaven Speaks to Those Who Do Not Know Jesus
Heaven Speaks to Those Who Are Dying
Heaven Speaks to Those Who Experience Tragedy
Heaven Speaks to Those Who Fear Purgatory
Heaven Speaks to Those Who Have Rejected God
Heaven Speaks to Those Who Struggle to Forgive
Heaven Speaks to Those Who Suffer from Financial Need
Heaven Speaks to Parents Who Worry About
　　Their Children's Salvation

All twenty of the "Heaven Speaks" booklets are now
available for free download and printing from our website
www.directionforourtimes.org. We encourage everyone to
print and distribute these booklets.

Other Written Works by Anne, a lay apostle

Climbing the Mountain

This book contains the fascinating story of how the rescue mission began and how it has blossomed into a worldwide apostolate under the watchful eye and in complete obedience to the Church. It is the story of The Lay Apostolate of Jesus Christ the Returning King.

Also featured is a summary of Anne's mystical experiences of heaven. She describes the heavenly home that has been created for God's children. Reading these accounts, you will learn that in heaven we will experience constant unity with Jesus. Anne also confirms that souls in heaven work together to assist in answering the prayers of God's earthly children. At one point in time Jesus tells Anne, *"...you are a child of God and you have every right to be here."*

In the section entitled "Climbing the Mountain," Anne writes about her vision of the personal call to holiness that we all must hear.

It concludes with a reprint of the first ten "Heaven Speaks" booklets: Abortion, Addictions, Victims of Clerical Abuse, Consecrated Souls, Depression, Divorce, Prisoners, Soldiers, Stress, and Young Adults.

This is a book to be treasured as it reveals the intimate love of the Savior for each soul. Every reader will be called to great rejoicing, for truly, God's Kingdom comes.

Serving in Clarity

This book could be described as the guidebook for lay apostles who wish to serve Jesus Christ the Returning King. In essence, it is the walking guide, given to us by heaven, describing how to obtain clarity so that our path up the Mountain of Holiness can be clearly identified.

The writing includes locutions from Jesus and Mary, encouraging us to trust that heaven is sending extraordinary graces so that we will say "yes" to helping Jesus usher in the Age of Obedience.

Anne then shares her insight on how we should live our lives in love, holiness and obedience to the Church. Aso included are vignettes of real life challenges that priests and people face while serving in their vocations.

Especially compelling is the description of Anne's mystical experiences of the Mountain of Holiness, where Jesus showed her the current condition of the world so that lay apostles would be encouraged to participate in God's rescue mission for souls.

Reprinted in this book is *In Defense of Obedience and Reflections on the Priesthood,* as well as the Monthly Messages from Jesus dated July 26 through June 2008.

Serving in Clarity is a gift for all those who are serious about learning God's will for their life.

In Defense of Obedience
and
Reflections on the Priesthood

This work by Anne consists of two essays on topics close to the heart of Jesus. The first is entitled *In Defense of Obedience* and the second is entitled *Reflections on the Priesthood.*

In Defense of Obedience is a serious call to return to a spirit of obedience to the Magisterium of the Church. Obedience to the Church is a must for every apostle, laity and clergy alike.

Anne's essay on the priesthood gives us the smallest glimpse of the love Our Lord has for the men who hear and answer His call. We read the depth of the connection Jesus has with these men and how they are united in a most unique way to the Sacred Heart of Jesus and the Immaculate Heart of Mary. This is also a gentle reminder that we are called to love and support our priests who serve us in their humanity but with a heavenly dignity bestowed upon them from heaven by Jesus Christ, the First Priest.

Interviews with Anne, a lay apostle

VHS tapes and DVDs featuring Anne, a lay apostle, have been produced by Focus Worldwide Network and can be purchased by visiting our website at:

www.directionforourtimes.org

This book is part of a non-profit mission.
Our Lord has requested that we
spread these words internationally.

Please help us.

If you would like to assist us financially,
please send your tax-deductible contribution
to the address below:

Direction for Our Times
9000 West 81st Street
Justice, Illinois 60458

www.directionforourtimes.org

Email: contactus@directionforourtimes.com
Phone: 708-496-9300

Direction for Our Times Ireland
Drumacarrow
Bailieborough
County Cavan.
Republic of Ireland

www.directionforourtimes.org

Email: contactus@dfot.ie
Phone: 353-(0)42-969-4947 or 353-(0)42-969-4734

Direction for Our Times is a 501(c)(3)
not-for-profit corporation. Contributions are
deductible to the extent provided by law.

Jesus gives Anne a message for the world on
the first of each month. To receive the
monthly messages you may access our
website at www.directionforourtimes.org
or call us at 708-496-9300
to be placed on our mailing list.